ALSO BY LAUREN GRAHAM

Someday, Someday, Maybe

Talking as Fast as I Can

· · · · · · · · · · · · · · · · · · · ·

LAUREN GRAHAM

· ·

Talking as Fast as I Can

From Gilmore Girls *to* Gilmore Girls,

(and Everything in Between)

BALLANTINE BOOKS

New York

Published in the United States by Ballantine Books, an imprint of
Random House, a division of Penguin Random House LLC, New York.

BALLANTINE and the HOUSE colophon are registered trademarks
of Penguin Random House LLC.

Grateful acknowledgment is made to the following for permission
to reprint previously published material:
Alfred Music and Hal Leonard LLC: Excerpt from "Slap that Bass"
(from *Shall We Dance*), music and lyrics by George Gershwin and Ira Gershwin, copyright © 1936 (renewed) Nokawi Music, Ira Gershwin Music, and
Frankie G. Songs. All rights for Nokawi Music administered by Imagem
Sounds. All rights for Ira Gershwin Music administered by WB Music Corp.
All rights for Frankie G. Sons administered by Songs Music Publishing. All
rights reserved. Used by permission of Alfred Music and Hal Leonard LLC.
Sony/ATV Music Publishing LLC: Excerpt from "The Trolley Song"
written by Ralph Blane and Hugh Martin, copyright © 1943 EMI Feist Cat-
alog Inc. All rights administered by Sony/ATV Music Publishing LLC, 424
Church Street, Suite 1200, Nashville, TN 37219. All rights reserved. Used by
permission of Sony/ATV Music Publishing LLC.

ISBN 978-0-425-28517-6
Ebook ISBN 978-0-425-28518-3

Printed in the United States of America on acid-free paper

randomhousebooks.com

4 6 8 9 7 5 3

Book design by Caroline Cunningham

for my mom and dad

Contents

. . . .

CONTENTS

Talking as Fast as I Can

. . . .

Introduction

. . . .

If you'd asked me back at the beginning of my career to guess which character I was most likely to return to, fifteen years after I'd played her for the first time, there would have been only one answer. Even back then I knew, from the very first time I read the script, that I had been given the opportunity to play someone very special. In fact, if you'd asked me to bet money on this guess, I would have bet every one of my pennies. Because even though I've been lucky enough to play many memorable ladies, and have true and deep affection for each and every person I've ever pretended to be, there's really only one with whom I have the most special kind of connection. In acting, as in life, you try to pretend you don't have favorites, but usually you do, and usually everyone else can see it too. I wrote this book because, luckily for me, my favorite was also a character beloved by fans and, in my opinion, represents the time I felt I was at my absolute best as an actor.

I think we can all agree I was never better, and the audience was never more impressed, than when I got the chance to inhabit this popular character:

The critics called me—well, I'm not sure we had a theater critic at Langley High School in the late 1980s. But I think it's undisputed that my performance as Dolly Gallagher Levi in *Hello, Dolly!* was indeed adored by fans, or, as I like to call them, my grandmother. I believe I'm quoting her verbatim, in fact, when I tell you she raved that my Dolly had "an impressive number of costume changes." And, not to brag, but my father also deemed my performance: "Wow, that hat sure has a lot of feathers." So I think I pretty much nailed everything there was to nail as an actress back in my junior year of high school. Which is why it's baffling that no one has yet called to invite me to reprise that role on Broadway, or even at the obvious next best place, the Langley High School auditorium. In fact—and I don't mean to sound like a diva here—I'm pretty upset about it. The People (my dad) DESERVE to see me again, years later, with (perhaps only slightly less) age makeup crayoned onto my face! Somebody get Ben Brantley on the phone! Watch your back, Carol Channing, I'm coming to get you!

But seriously.

I *really* wrote this book because getting to play fast-talking Lorelai Gilmore again made me reflect on what it had been like to play her the first time, and that made me reflect on how I even got there at all, and some of the ways my life had changed in between the first and second incarnations. So this book is about the past, and also the (almost) present, since I'll share with you some of the diary I kept while filming *Gilmore Girls: A Year in the Life*.

In this book, I will also see into the future and report my findings to you and to select heads of state. These findings will be lies, as I cannot actually see into the future, but who can stop me saying whatever I want here? It's *my* book! I'm drunk with power!

This book is about growing up, starting out, and the time I was asked to audition with my butt. It's about all the odd jobs I had on the way to pursuing my dream, some of the bad fashion choices I made, and the eleventy million diets I've tried. I'll tell you how I learned to be a more efficient writer, how I discovered that I'm a terrible judge, and how I realized that meeting guys at awards shows was perhaps not the best way to start a successful relationship.

I wondered what it would be like to put someone I loved so much down for eight years and then pick her up again. I wondered if rebooting *Gilmore Girls* could be as gratifying as doing the series was the first time, if the show would feel as fresh and quirky and smart and speedy as it had been, if returning to Stars Hollow after all those years would be as wonderful as I'd dreamed it would be.

Spoiler alert: it was.

Fast Forward

. . . .

Some of the most exciting things that happened in my life took place before I turned six years old. I was born in Honolulu, Hawaii, which is awesome right there, but three weeks later, before I even had time to work on my tan, we moved to Japan. JAPAN. The home of my most favorite food ever: mashed peas. Well, that was probably my favorite food back then; what a waste, since I could have been eating spicy tuna rolls with extra wasabi. Damn you, Baby Lauren, and your infantile palate! Well, to be fair, you *were* an infant. Sorry I yelled.

In Tokyo, we lived with my grandmother for a while, and I had a Japanese nanny, or *uba*—which, incidentally, translates to "milk mother," something I just found out by looking it up. (Hold, please, while I call my therapist.) Her name was Sato-san, and I loved her, and as a result, my first word was in Japanese. It was *o-heso*. You might think that's Japanese for "mommy" or "daddy," but no, *o-heso* is Japanese for "belly button," which I think already proves I am a very unusual, deep, and contemplative person and there's really nothing left to say, thank you for buying this book, the end.

Wait, a few more things. My mother, the daughter of missionaries, had grown up in Japan and spoke fluent Japanese. She was also incredibly smart and beautiful, a combination that led to this:

That's my grandmother holding me while we watch my mother, who is *on television*! Back when there were just three channels in America, and maybe even fewer in Tokyo, and an air of mystery surrounding the whole thing—not like today, when the statistical probability of *not* at some point stumbling onto your own reality show is inconceivably low. Television had only recently been *invented* then, and there she was actually on it, and I was so little I was probably just thinking about mashed peas again. Or, more likely, my favorite subject: belly buttons.

In related news, apparently on some GikiWoogle-type

page of mine, I am quoted as saying, "Belly buttons are important." Which, while obviously sort of true, medically speaking, taking into account the life-giving properties of the umbilical cord, was also clearly a joke. Yet I can't tell you how many times during an interview a journalist gets that somber I'm-going-in-for-the-kill look I love so much and asks me, with knitted-brow faux sincerity: "Do you *really* think belly buttons are important?" Let me clear the air once and for all: um, no, I do not. Although this book isn't very long yet and I've already talked about belly buttons quite a bit. Damn you, tabloid journalists! You wise Truth Uncoverers! Again, sorry—the yelling must stop.

So, anyway, there she was, my mother, on the largest television available at the time, which was roughly the size of a Rubik's cube. Also, check out her dope sixties Priscilla Presley look! Her ability to speak the language as a non-native was so unusual at the time that she was asked to appear on a Japanese daytime talk show.

My parents weren't together very long. They hadn't known each other well when they decided to get married, and then they had me right away, when they were both just twenty-two years old, and—well, that about sums it up. They were very, very young. At the time, my mom was also trying to pursue a career as a singer, and it was decided I should stay with my dad. They parted as friends, and my father made the obvious next choice, something we'd all probably do in this situation: he moved us to the Virgin Islands, where we lived on a houseboat. I slept in a bunk-bed-type thing that was also the kitchen. I was picked up for nursery school by the bus, which was actually a motorboat. We moved there because . . .

You know what? I don't remember exactly. Let's call my dad and ask him. He probably won't pick up because he's on the East Coast, and it's a Saturday in the springtime, so unless it's pouring down rain, he's out playing golf. But I'll give you a visual just in case, so you too can play Call My Dad at home!

I know, isn't it a shame we look nothing alike? Okay, let's see if he's home.

Ring, ring, ring, ring.

I told you. He's probably not—

DAD: Hello?

ME: Oh, hi! I didn't think you'd be home.

DAD: It's raining here.

ME: Well, then, that explains it. Hey, remind me—why did we live on a houseboat that time?

DAD: Who is this?

ME: You have other children you lived on a houseboat with?

DAD: No, I have other children who call me more.

ME: Dad, please. I call you all the time. So this is for the book, and—

DAD: Is this going to be another befuddled father character, like in your last book?

ME: Dad, I wouldn't call that character befuddled in general. He's just a little befuddled by *technology.*

DAD: Wait—what did you say? I couldn't hear you. I just hit one of these dumb phone buttons wrong.

ME: Um, yeah. I was just saying that the father character in my first novel—the *New York Times* bestseller *Someday, Someday, Maybe,* published by Ballantine Books, an imprint of Random House, and now available in paperback—is not exactly *befuddled,* and anyway, he's only a little bit you.

DAD: Why are you talking like that?

ME: Like what? I was just thinking about how Christmas is right around the corner, but no matter how you choose to celebrate the holidays, books in general make great gifts!

DAD: Like that. Like you're selling things to an audience. Are you on *Ellen* right now?

ME: Dad, I wouldn't be calling you from the set of *Ellen.*

DAD: Oh, oh, I'm *fancy,* I live in *Hollywood,* where people aren't allowed to call their fathers from the set of the *Ellen* show.

ME: Dad, please. Why did we live on the houseboat again?

DAD: Well, I was working for that congressman, and
the hours were long, and I'd drop you off in the
morning and not see you until after 6:00 p.m., and
I felt bad about that. I wasn't sure I was on the
right career path anyway. Also, I was sort of seeing
this girl—you remember the one who owned the
horse? Well, she lived there off and on, and I
thought I'd go there too, and write, and . . .

I'm going to interrupt my father here (well, actually, he's
still talking, so shhh—don't tell him). But I have to explain to
you that, as a kid, I thought my father never dated anyone at
all until he met and married my stepmother. It wasn't until
years later that I figured out the young ladies who sometimes
came around may have been a wee bit more than the "cat sit-
ter," that "nice woman I play tennis with," and the "girl who
owned the horse." And I don't blame them. I mean, who
wouldn't want to "cat-sit" for this guy?

By the way, can we talk about the unnecessary thickness of children's belts of the 1970s? I mean look at the— Oops, my dad's still on the phone!

DAD: ... and anyway, she knew these people at the marina in St. Thomas.

ME: So did we, like, sail around the island and stuff?

DAD: Oh, no. The engine didn't work on the boat.

ME: The engine didn't ... ? We lived on a giant floating bathtub that went nowhere?

DAD: It was a strange place, I'll admit, that marina— but friendly. Very bohemian. Everybody there was sort of dropping out from society, which we were too, in a way—for weeks after we'd left D.C., I'm pretty sure my mother still thought I worked on Capitol Hill. But I got to spend more time with you, which was the goal. It was beautiful there. We drove around a lot and went to the beach. It probably seems strange to you now, but it was a 1970s thing to do, I guess. And we had fun.

(A pause as we both reminisce.)

ME: You did a lot for me, Dad. I love you.

DAD: I love you too, kid.

(Another pause.)

DAD: *Who* is this again?

When I was about five years old, we moved to Southampton, New York, presumably to live in a house you couldn't dive off of, and I started kindergarten. One day, during my first few weeks of school, the teacher left the room (leaving youngsters alone with open jars of paste was also very 1970s), and when she came back, she found me reading a book to the class. At first she thought maybe I'd memorized it from having it read to me at home, but after I wowed them with a cold read of another one—take that, *Green Eggs and Ham!*—they had to admit I could actually read. My father had read to me every night for as long as I could remember, and at some point, I guess, I just sort of got it. But this confused the teacher and the school, because I'd unintentionally undermined their entire plan for the year. If I wasn't in kindergarten to be taught to read, could they really justify sharing and finger painting as a comprehensive year-long curriculum? If not, what were they supposed to do with me?

I was sent to the office of a groovy guy named Mike. I don't know what Mike's actual job at the school was, but I remember sitting in his office drawing pictures of my feelings or whatever (the seventies!), while he leaned back in his chair with his feet up on the desk, which is how I knew he was groovy in the first place. This went on for days. Mike kept asking me if I was bored in kindergarten. Not really, Mike— have you seen the awesome books they have in there? And that's about all I remember. But by the end of the week, I had apparently convinced Mike that making chains out of construction paper for an entire year would be beneath me intellectually, and he sent me on to first grade.

During my first day in the new class, the teacher held a mock election and asked each student to come up and mark on the blackboard whom they'd vote for in the upcoming presidential election: McGovern or Nixon (the seventies!). McGovern won by a landslide (not in real life but, weirdly, in this class), and I was one of very few kids who voted for Nixon. This gave me an uneasy feeling. Even though I had no idea who either of the candidates was, or even what the word "candidate" meant, I knew that in not being part of the majority, I'd somehow made the wrong choice. Also, how could the entire room *not* vote for a guy named Nixon, because seriously, how cool was it to have the letter x in your name? That this distinguishing feature didn't similarly blow everyone else's mind the way it did mine was my first indication that I was in over my head.

Initially, skipping a grade seemed like an accomplishment of some sort, but what I remember most was how totally baffled and uncomfortable I felt, especially for the first few weeks. I'd never really had trouble fitting in before, and now, instead of feeling special or gifted, I just felt awkward and out of place. Suddenly this thing that had made me stand out and had impressed some people now made me feel like an odd-ball.

But skipping a grade also gave me the sense, throughout my entire childhood, that I'd been given an "extra" year. It floated around in my head like a lucky coin, something I wanted to hold on to as long as I could, until the day I really needed to use it. I don't know why exactly, but somehow I got the idea that life was just a massive competition to get to some sort of finish line, like one long extended season of *The Amazing Race*. In skipping a grade, I'd been given the ultimate Fast Forward. This would ensure I'd be able to skip over whatever the life equivalent is of the shemozzle race in New Zealand, beating out even the most awesome teams like the Twinnies or the Afghanimals, then arrive first and be met by an adorable gnome, an oversized cardboard check for a million dollars from Phil, and a trip from Travelocity.

There were a few years in there where I mostly forgot about the whole skipping-a-grade thing. In elementary and middle school I spent time riding horses every weekend, sometimes working in a barn after school, and having birthday slumber parties during which we'd sneak out in the middle of the night to go pajama streaking. (We're running! Around the block! In our pajamas! The excitement!) I also enjoyed such sophisticated pastimes as toilet-papering people's houses (this wasn't necessarily a *bad* thing in my group of friends—in fact, it was a good sign if people cared enough to TP your house; I remember praying I'd be TP'd *more*), acting out elaborate soap operas involving my troll dolls, making horse blankets for my thirty-seven Breyer horses, and recording Judy Garland movies off the television with my red plastic Radio Shack tape recorder. I'd stay up late, listening to my cassette tapes over and over, which is why I'm happy to announce I can still perform "The Trolley Song" for you right now!

> *With my high starched collar,*
> *And my high-top shoes,*
> *And my hair piled high upon—*

What's that? Oh, okay, you're probably right, let's do it later.

Anyway, my dad met my stepmother around this time, and they got married, and we moved farther out into the suburbs of Virginia, partly so I'd be closer to the barn where I rode, which was ironic since it wouldn't be long before I'd replace all the time I'd been spending there with all the time I'd spend doing school plays.

Skipping a grade came up again during my sophomore year of high school, when everyone but me started getting their driver's license. I wanted off the school bus badly, and not being able to drive until later than everyone else seemed an unfair penalty for being able to read a little bit before them.

The drinking age in Virginia was twenty-one, but just over the bridge in D.C. it was only eighteen, and we heard that fake IDs worked there with surprising regularity. Our desire to get into the bars in Georgetown was due mainly to a wish to be able to dance for hours with the music turned up to volumes that weren't allowed in our suburban basements. This was during a time in high school when dancing was in fashion. There came a day when dancing suddenly went away, when it simply wasn't cool anymore. But during that time it was mysteriously deemed okay, and I remember all of us happily jumping around like freaks for any reason at all. Michael Jackson moonwalked on TV, and no one had seen or heard anything like him. With the top of her convertible VW Rabbit down, Virginia Rowan and I yelled along to Wham! and Morrisey and a new singer named Madonna. Bruce Springsteen was everything then. My friend Kathryn Donnelly would regularly get up on a table and sing every word of "Born to Run," using a broom handle as her microphone. Musically, it was a great time to be a teenager.

I wasn't interested in drinking at the time, but some of the other girls were, and everyone was petrified of getting pulled over. So that's how I, at fifteen and without a license, was chosen to be the regular designated driver of Joyce Antonio's father's Mercedes. This made perfect sense to me as fair payment for having to suffer through the injustice of being a year younger than everyone else. My friends who wanted to drink were covered. Everybody won!

AHAHAHAHA, what a TERRIBLE idea this was. Literally the worst example of "learning by doing" ever. But I remember all of us thinking it was a really wise and grown-up choice, and feeling very proud of ourselves for figuring out this genius way to solve our need-to-dance-while-drinking-illegally problem. Because really, aren't laws actually just pesky suggestions? Who needs them? Fifteen-year-olds know everything! The good news was that we'd taken the "Don't Drink and Drive" campaign seriously. The bad news was that the "Don't Get on the Road If You Aren't a Licensed Driver" campaign just didn't have as catchy a slogan. In fact, driving without a license was such a dumb idea, I doubt it had even occurred to anyone to start an ad campaign about how dumb it was.

Miraculously, we all lived. And eventually I got my license. During the driving part of the test, I worried that my ability to parallel-park on the first try would raise eyebrows, and the instructor would turn to me and say, "I have a suspicion you know how to do this because of all the time you spent sneaking into Winston's with a fake ID so you could dance all night to 'PYT.'" Lucky for me, he didn't.

Throughout all of this, my free year was still on my mind, and I was so intent on saving it for the "right" time that I missed an opportunity where it actually might have been helpful. I spent my freshman year in the undergraduate acting program at NYU's Tisch School of the Arts. It is and was a wonderful program, and I had some great teachers, but at just seventeen years old, I felt lost, and doing things like sitting in a chair for hours attempting to summon feelings of "cold" and "hot" wasn't what I'd envisioned college to be. I visited friends at other, more academic programs, and worried I was missing out. So at the end of the year, I transferred to Barnard College to be an English major.

Not surprisingly, my Temperatures class, among others, didn't have much value at my new school, and almost none of my credits transferred. This would have been a wonderful time to start over as a freshman, but I wasn't ready to let go of my lucky penny just yet! So in order to graduate on time, I had to take a full academic load every semester. To that, I added plays and musicals, and the a cappella group the Metrotones, which toured other colleges most weekends. I was completely overwhelmed and behind on my studies for three years straight. Barnard College has been very good to me, and I love going back to speak there or just to visit, but I'm sure they've (rightly) buried my transcript somewhere far below the 1 train at 116th Street and Broadway.

The year after I graduated from college ended up being the moment when I finally plunked my lucky penny down on the table. Most people would just call this "the year after I graduated from college," but to me, it became the withdrawal on the time I'd put in the bank in my head.

My best friends from school all either had gone abroad, had gotten jobs somewhere besides New York, or had a year of school left. So without any of my buddies to share a place with, I lived in a tiny room in an apartment that faced an airshaft. Somehow, given my pretty limited and lackluster wardrobe, I was hired at a clothing store where I worked during the day. At night I got a job as a cocktail waitress. My days usually started before 8:00 a.m. and I'd get home after 2:00 a.m., dead on my feet but facing the same hours the next day. Even so, I didn't earn enough money to have much to live on after I paid my rent.

Also, I realized that while I'd spent almost my entire time in school and in the summers being involved in some sort of performing arts, I was now living a life without any of them. Even when I was broke back in college, I was acting or singing in a million productions, and could always find a way to see plays and musicals too: volunteer as an usher, maybe, or get discounted tickets through the student store. Now, though, I had neither the time nor the money to see anything, let alone *be* in anything. Worried I'd get rusty, I had to resort to standing in the center of my living room/kitchen/bedroom facing the airshaft at three in the morning practicing scales.

Which reminds me—

> *Iiiiiiii went to lose a jolly*
> *Hour on the trolley*
> *And lost my heart ins—*

Really? You *still* don't want to hear it? Oh, you're worried about the neighbors in my New York apartment building back then? Hmmm. I never met them, but from what I remember, the people upstairs sounded like they were running a cat hotel while training for Riverdance. But okay, let's wait.

The months ticked by, and I became more and more worried. It was one thing to feel the extra year slipping away, but something worse had begun to occur to me. What if one year turned into two, and two turned into "Poor Aunt Melba can't come for Christmas this year, Billy, she's working a double shift again"? I'm not sure how my name got changed to Melba in this negative fantasy, but the way things were heading then, anything could happen!

I felt trapped. And I felt dumb. I obviously hadn't used my lucky penny at the right time, and now I had no edge, nothing that separated me from any other struggling sap in the city. What was I going to do? Drop everything and move to an engineless houseboat in a harbor in St. Thomas? This wasn't "go find yourself" 1972 anymore! It was 1989, and the belts were way thinner!

At a loss, I signed up to participate in what was called the URTAs, a yearly audition held in New York by a consortium of graduate programs in the arts. Since these schools were located all over the country, they sent representatives to New York to recruit actors once a year. As my potential new life plan, this made no sense. I was still heavily in debt from undergrad, so paying for graduate school wasn't an option at all. Plus, moving anywhere else seemed counterintuitive. I'd dreamed my whole life of making it in New York City, and I'd made it! Well, I resided there, at least. Now I was going to, what—move to *Denver*? It seemed I was getting further away from my dream, not closer to it. But there was only a month left on my apartment lease, and I had to make some decisions. Would I stay or would I go?

To be at the audition, I had to take time off from work I couldn't afford. I was asked to prepare a classical monologue, a contemporary monologue, and a song. I spent any free hours I had at the Lincoln Center performing arts library, listening to cast albums and reading plays. I had no coach or teacher or really anyone to try my material out on. In the end, I blindly chose an odd assortment: Linda from *Savage in Limbo* by John Patrick Shanley, Rosalind from *As You Like It,* and "Somewhere That's Green" from *Little Shop of Horrors.* I had nowhere to rehearse, no time to prepare. I'd go to sleep after twelve hours on my feet just reciting the lines in my head. The audition was held in a slightly spooky old theater in Times Square. I'd hardly even done the pieces out loud before. The stage was massive—I'd never performed in a space so huge—and my voice sounded thin. The audience was unresponsive.

But somehow I got in.

I was actually accepted to a few places, but at Southern Methodist University I was offered something I didn't even know existed: a full scholarship to their Meadows School for the Arts. I mean, who in their right mind would offer to pay for actors to become actors? Bob Hope, that's who! There's a whole theater there named after him, and in general it's a very wealthy school. But I'd never dreamed of such a miraculous thing. I felt relieved to have a new path, and vindicated to still be on track. I wasn't ahead, but at least I was normal! Going to graduate school at normal-people times!

Except that when I got there, I realized that there *was* no normal. There were students from all over the place, all of them different ages and at various stages of their lives and careers. This was shocking to me. Didn't they know the clock was ticking? Weren't they worried about getting the first tuk-tuk in Bangkok?

Apparently they were not.

I also discovered that being away from New York at a more traditionally collegiate school had its merits and its comforts. I lived in a sprawling apartment complex with new wall-to-wall carpeting and a pool. I got to focus on being a performer without having to worry about my academics or the basics of surviving in the city—something I didn't have that first year at NYU. I had an incredible acting teacher, Cecil O'Neal. I made great friends. We laughed a lot, loved each other, and tortured each other as only a close-knit company of actors knows how to do. There was a guy in the class ahead of us who nicknamed everyone's heads, for example, according to what they reminded him of. Members of our class were named "Pumpkin Head," "Pencil-Eraser Head," and "Punched-In Football Head," among others. I was dubbed "Hair Head"; I can't imagine why.

I still find that, in general, having a plan is, well, a good plan. But when my carefully laid plan laughed at me, rather than clutch at it too tightly I just made a new one, even if it was one that didn't immediately make sense. In blindly trying a different path, I accidentally found one that worked better. So don't let your plan have the last laugh, but laugh last when your plan laughs, and when your plan has the last laugh, laugh back, laughing!

People always ask me how I got to be an actor. The good news and the bad news is: there is no one way. That I thought I had some sort of leg up on life or my career by bartering my perceived time chip was an illusion. In life, of course, there is no Fast Forward. Fast Forward doesn't even always work on *The Amazing Race.* Half the time the team in first place makes it onto the earliest flight to a new city, thinking they're ahead, and arrives at the next destination only to find it doesn't open for two more hours. Then the other teams catch up, evening the playing field once more. On *The Amazing Race,* this might mean you lose a million dollars. But in life, maybe it's actually . . . fine? Because who wants to Fast Forward anyway? You might miss some of the good parts. I'd rather keep pushing the rewind button on my red Radio Shack tape recorder and be that geek who knows the lyrics to the songs from every Judy Garland musical ever.

Oh, really? Now's a good time? Oh, good! Here goes. . . .

Clang clang clang went the trolley . . .

Sweat Equity

. . . .

For some reason I had very old-timey ideas about what show business was like when I was first starting out. Maybe it was all those afternoons I spent watching *The 4:30 Movie* when I was supposed to be doing my homework. (Sorry, Dad!) Back then, there weren't many ways to learn about what the life of a working actor was actually like, or even get a glimpse into how to get started. Pre–*American Idol,* the closest thing we had to a show business competition was *Star Search,* but the acting portion was oddly stiff and theatrical, and never seemed very authentic. The world of entertainment-related periodicals was different then too: there weren't fifteen gossip publications like there are today, all of them competing to be the first to tell you where J. Lo had dinner last night or to reveal the name of Kate Hudson's new bichon frise. The *National En-quirer* spent some time on the secret world of celebrities, but focused equally on alien babies and Loch Ness monster sightings. There was no *Real Housewives* of anywhere, and no Twitter or Instagram or Snapchat, where people could constantly update you on their every move. People—even famous people—had not yet begun to focus on their "brands," and there was really only one daily show about Hollywood, *Entertainment Tonight,* which was pretty fluffy back then, and fairly tame. Magazines were not yet going after every detail of what went on behind the scenes. No one was asking the important questions of today, like "Whose cellulite is this?"

The 4:30 Movie featured mostly old films and was categorized around a weekly theme: Elvis week, Westerns week, horror week, etc. That's where I fell in love with movie musicals starring Gene Kelly and Judy Garland. That's where I decided Katharine Hepburn was my favorite actress of all time. That's where I learned that an actor's highest calling was The Theatah and the ultimate goal for a true thespian was BroadWAY, emphasis on the WAY. I was inspired by the black-and-white movies of the 1930s and 1940s, like *Stage Door,* in which young hopefuls lived together in a sorority-type house, sleeping with their hair in old-fashioned curlers that looked more like rags, practicing dance steps in their tiny galley kitchen while wearing silk tap pants and dreaming of Broad-WAY. I loved their vivid vernacular and tried to incorporate it into my life. "Say, fella, this gal's got sore gams," I was in the habit of saying. "My dogs are barking—got a dime for a cup of joe?" This being the mid-eighties, no one had any idea what I was talking about.

I was determined to make it to BroadWAY, and that meant I somehow had to become a member of Actors' Equity, the theatrical union. The union conundrum: you can't get a union card without getting a union job, and you can't get a union job unless you're in the union. My plan, although the path was long, was to earn enough hours as an Equity apprentice to become eligible, which could take years. The only faster way would be to somehow get cast in an Equity role. Apparently this happened once in a while, when a part called for something unique that none of the members of the Equity company were able to do. As a young actor, I remember focusing obsessively on the "special skills" section of my résumé, peppering it with abilities, even ones I only sort of had, in case one of them might lead to my big break. Included on my résumé at the time were "skills" such as driving (not a given in New York City), roller skating (the musical *Starlight Express* was big at the time), dialects (although this claim was vague and pretty much untrue, I felt it made me seem sophisticated and Shakespearean), and Rhonda Weiss impressions (Rhonda Weiss was one of my favorite characters from Gilda Radner's *Live at Carnegie Hall* show, a VHS tape I watched obsessively). Why I thought anyone would be more impressed by *my* Rhonda Weiss than by Gilda Radner's is still an embarrassing mystery to me today. But back then, especially when coupled with dialects and driving, I thought it made me seem quirky and well-rounded. Probably despite these skills rather than because of them, I landed a spot in the Equity apprentice program at the Barn Theater in Augusta, Michigan.

The Barn was (and is) a well-respected summer theater that had a resident Equity company and even occasionally drew some Broadway stars. In the lobby of the theater hung framed headshots of "Barnies" of note—actors who'd once been apprentices here, just like I was, and had gone on to bigger things. I didn't recognize any of their faces, but I was still impressed. It was beyond my wildest hope that my headshot would one day hang in this lobby too, prompting scores of theatergoers to remark, "Who?" I could only dream of such obscurity!

On the first day at the Barn, all the Equity apprentices auditioned for the directors and members of the Equity company to get their specific casting for the summer. The core Equity company consisted of experienced actors, most from New York, who'd been hired for the whole summer. Many of them had worked at the theater before, and they all knew each other. They asked me a few questions, then chose a piece for me to sight-read: "Slap That Bass," a Gershwin number from the musical *Crazy for You*. I didn't know the song, but the whole point was to see how well we could perform with limited preparation. The rehearsal period for each show was only two weeks, so it was important to show them how quickly we could learn music and dance steps. I was nervous but not too worried, since in general I could sight-read pretty well.

Or so I thought.

Even though I was only expected to read off sheet music on the stand in front of me, I wanted to really perform the song, to prove I was not only a speedy learner and a good singer but a good actress too. My casting for the entire season depended on what I did in this audition. The pianist played through a few bars and hummed the melody for me until I felt ready to try the song alone. Then I took a deep breath and started to sing.

Zoom zoom zoom zoom
The world is in a mess
With politics and taxes
And people grinding axes
There's no happiness.

Looking out at the sea of faces in the audience, I could tell right away that I was doing well. I felt relaxed and my voice sounded strong. People were smiling and tapping their toes to the beat.

Zoom zoom zoom zoom
Rhythm lead your ace
The future doesn't fret me
If I can only get me
Someone to slap that bass.

I saw one of the Equity actors in the audience exchange a look with the music director. She clapped her hand over her mouth like she was stifling a laugh. He giggled back at her and slapped his knee, and I thought, wow—are they impressed or what? It's almost as if they've never seen an apprentice perform this well on their first day. I wondered briefly if I had a chance at getting my Equity card in my first summer. I'd been told that *never* happened, but what if? They'd talk about it for years to come! Not only would my headshot be displayed in the lobby, but maybe they'd need a plaque touting my incredible accomplishment as well! APPRENTICE FOR A DAY. THEN STRAIGHT TO BROAD*WAY*, it would say! A wave of extra confidence washed over me, hurtling me toward the chorus:

Slap that bass
Slap it till it's dizzy
Slap that bass
Keep the rhythm busy
Zoom zoom zoom
Misery, you've got to go!

Everyone in the audience was laughing now, and I thought, well, that's sort of weird, but they aren't stopping me, and they all look pretty pleased. The problem was that they looked almost *too* pleased. I hadn't really seen "Slap That Bass" as much of a comedic song, but maybe I was wrong? So I decided to go with their response and sort of shimmied my shoulders, adding even more personality and pizzazz.

Slap that bass
Use it like a tonic
Slap that bass
Keep your philharmonic
Zoom zoom zoom
And the milk and honey'll flow!

There was no doubting it now—everyone was now becoming almost . . . hysterical? One of the actresses was wiping tears away, she was laughing so hard. I'm just naturally funny, I guess, I thought. I never realized it to this degree before. This is for sure the day I'll be discovered! Never mind my promotion to the Equity company—maybe I won't even last the summer here! What if they send me directly to Broad-WAY? I wondered if I'd have to drop out of Barnard, and if not, how I would manage both my schoolwork and my full-time stardom. Flush with the excitement of my newfound destiny, I beamed back at them all and headed into my big finish:

> *In which case*
> *If you want a bauble*
> *Slap that bass*
> *Slap away your trouble*
> *Learn to zoom zoom zoom*
> *Slap that bass!*

Arms outstretched, I held the last note as long as I could. The entire room applauded, I bowed, and then they all dissolved into giggles. For a while they were laughing so hard that no one could speak. Finally the music director waved his arm over his head, signaling everyone to be quiet.

"Lauren," he said kindly, "you have a good voice."

A *good* voice? Didn't he mean a spectacular, transcendent, unique, miracle voice from Heavenland?

"A very good voice," he said, and paused. I could tell he was struggling to keep a straight face. "But I don't think Ira Gershwin wrote this song about a fish."

For a moment I felt surrounded by fog, or like I'd just been woken up from a deep sleep. What was he talking about? *What* about a fish? Why would he—

And then it hit me.

In my haste to show how quickly I could learn the song, I hadn't really stopped to consider what the song was *about,* which was someone joyously playing the bass fiddle. I mean,

I sort of knew that, but in my nervousness, I didn't pronounce "bass" like the instrument—like "face," "place," or even "ace," a word that was *actually in the song*. I pronounced it like "pass," "grass," or "ass"—which was also what I now felt like. Fueled by adrenaline and dreams of my Equity card, I'd turned a song about playing an instrument into a song about abusing a fish. Over and over, I'd just gleefully sung about hitting the poor fishy upside the head. I'd given "slapping a bass" a whole new meaning. No wonder they were laughing so hard.

In my mind's eye, I removed my framed headshot from the theater lobby. My plaque faded into the wings. My Equity card evaporated in the glare of the footlights.

But eventually I recovered, and managed to get into the summer stock routine. The apprentices worked very, very hard. In addition to rehearsing during the afternoon, our duties included anything and everything it took to keep the theater going, including costume sewing, set building, and floor mopping. Mornings were spent doing chores like cleaning the bathrooms and painting the fence that surrounded the property. I lucked out and for a few weeks got a coveted job working in the box office taking ticket orders over the phone. The box office was luxurious compared to the outdoor activities we performed in the 100-degree heat. It had both air-conditioning and a constant influx of baked goods from the theater-loving locals. The baked goods were supposed to be sent directly to the Equity actors, but most never made it past whoever was manning the phones. Every day I'd have stolen cakes and cookies for breakfast, a Chinese chicken salad from McDonald's for lunch (do they still make this? It was *so* good), and then came "dinner," or what passed for dinner on an apprentice's nonexistent salary, a combination of food and beverage that I loved more than I've loved some meals I've had at restaurants with Michelin stars. I'll tell you what it was in a second, but I warn you—it appeals only to those with the most discerning palates.

After the main stage shows, there was a sort of bar that opened next door to the theater called the Shed, where the apprentices performed cabaret-type songs and skits for any audience members who didn't yet want to call it a night. On the main stage we were chorus members, bit players at best, but at the Shed show afterward, we were the stars. I personally wowed audiences by accompanying myself on songs with the acoustic guitar I'd brought from home, my greatness limited only by my dreams and the fact that I knew how to play just three chords. But that's all you need for "Leaving on a Jet Plane," my friends! At the Shed, the "stars" were also the waiters, so the storeroom in the back doubled as our back-stage area and locker room. It was a chaotic jumble of costume pieces for our upcoming numbers, bar supplies, and personal stuff. The back room was also where they kept the Snak-Ens, an evil mix of delicious seasoned crackers and pretzels that I'm pretty sure the dastardly Gardetto's company invented in an attempt to ruin my career, even though at the time I had no career to speak of. We weren't allowed to indulge in the Snak-Ens, which were kept in giant garbage-bin-sized tubs in the storeroom—those were only for the PAYING CUSTOMERS. The theater owners were VERY strict about this. So I'm here to tell you, and any former employers (or health inspectors) who may be reading this, that we 100 percent DID NOT reach our grubby hands into the giant bins

OVER AND OVER every night until we were sick with salt bloat. How DARE you imply such a thing! That summer, I also discovered the first alcoholic drink I actually liked the taste of, a drink that was very hip and happening at the time, and is still a sign of intellect and sophistication. I'm talking, of course, about the Fuzzy Navel. This nutrient-packed, classy combination of Snak-Ens and Fuzzy Navels was my dinner for two whole months.

Halfway through the summer, an incredible opportunity came up. An Equity part was going to be given to one of the apprentices. It was a smallish part, so to bring an Equity actor all the way from New York would be too costly. It was cheaper to just give one of the apprentices their card and pay them Equity wages for the two-week run. This was exactly the scenario I'd imagined, precisely the break I'd been hoping for! There was much excitement and discussion among the apprentices about the part, and also about what it required. The play was a farce, a broad comedy about two cheating husbands and the wives they're lying to, and the role was a French maid that one of the husbands is caught having an affair with. When the maid and the husband are discovered in bed, the maid stands up in fright, and as she's facing upstage, babbling in French, the blanket that's been covering her falls, exposing her bare backside to the audience.

The rumor was that the director would only be bringing a few girls in to audition, and we wondered nervously whom he'd choose. The next day, a short list was posted, and my name was on it. I was thrilled and flattered. We then learned that the entire audition would consist of being brought into a room and showing our bare butts to the director. I wasn't sure exactly how that would work (enter walking backward?), and I thought it was a little odd that we weren't being asked to read even a small part of the actual scene, but I was still both thrilled and flattered. This was the sort of thing professional actresses were asked to do all the time. My Equity card was just a bare-butt-flash away!

The Chosen Butts became an instant club of sorts. We tried our best to be professional and not act overly excited, but it was clear we were bonded because of our excellent butts I mean acting ability. We didn't want those of lesser butt to feel left out, but we'd subtly smile at each other in the hallways, pleased at having been singled out for our shapely butts I mean talent. The phrase "butt buddies" had never made so much sense!

The day of the audition came. We were asked to disrobe from the waist down in private, and when we were ready, two girls holding a sheet walked out slightly in front of us. We walked up behind them and turned around, the girls dropped the sheet for a brief moment for the director, then they put it back up and we all walked out together. During the entrance and exit, the director made innocuous small talk. His wife was sitting beside him, there to ensure we were comfortable. Everyone was very respectful. The whole thing was over so quickly, I barely had time to register any feelings about it at all. I walked out smiling, waved to the rest of my BBs, who were waiting to go in, got dressed, and went to a secluded place behind the theater, where I burst into tears.

There was nothing wrong with the way anyone con-

ducted themselves that day. The audition process was thought-
fully executed. The play was silly and full of sexual innuendo,
and nudity was called for in the script.

I just didn't like it.

The audition made me feel vulnerable and just plain bad
about myself. On top of that, I was embarrassed not to have
thought the whole thing through more thoroughly. I wanted
my Equity card so desperately, I hadn't stopped to ask myself
what I was comfortable doing in order to get it. In art, the
painter presents his canvas. In acting, the canvas is you. Over
the years, I've learned to have a sort of distance from myself in
certain situations—I've regularly stripped down to nothing in
front of a stranger in order to have a fitting, for example. As
actors, we are poked and prodded by other artists whose con-
tributions are vital to presenting the canvas at its best: hair,
makeup, lighting, scenery. The canvas is given lines to say,
someone else's clothes to wear. In acting you have to have an
objectivity that enables you to, at times, turn yourself over to
someone else and let them do the painting. But this was my
first experience paying more attention to the canvas part than
the me part, and I realized both sides needed to line up. I'd
thought it was mature and professional to do anything asked
of me to get the job. I learned a little too late that day that
maybe it was more complex than that.

The girl who got the part was an apprentice in her second or third year, a great comedienne with a great figure. She
had no problem being semi-naked in rehearsals and seemed
to really enjoy doing the show every night. There's a lid for
every pot, they say, and there's definitely an actor for every
role (and then some). The truth was, even if I'd gotten it, that

part just wasn't a good fit. The me of today often reads scripts I don't connect with, and I've learned not to worry about it too much. If a story doesn't resonate with me—even if it's a really good one, even if it's one I wish I could be part of— I just have to accept that I probably wouldn't be as compelling as someone else could be in the role. And it's become fairly easy to let them go.

One of my incredible acting teachers, Wynn Handman, always talked about how important it was to have a feel for the material. He dismissed the idea that every actor should be able to tackle every part. "Charlie Chaplin did just one thing," he'd say. "He just did it better than everyone else." Later on, I'd learn not to feel too bad when I realized a part wasn't right for me. But at that young age, with only high school and college plays on my résumé, I didn't think I had any right to be choosy or to have much of an opinion about what I wanted to do. At the time, I had only the vaguest hint that my instincts might be worth respecting.

It would take many more years to learn how best to respond to those instincts. But when, during the course of my early career, I was asked a few more times about nudity, the answer was always a fairly easy no. Nothing wrong with it, and a vital part of some kinds of storytelling; just not for me.

In my second summer at the Barn, I was given an Equity role without even having to audition for it. I was *chosen*. This was a real honor, and a very big deal among the other apprentices, and it happened so much earlier than I thought it would. My headshot plaque dreams returned! The character was named Marjorie Baverstock, and the play was called *The Musical Comedy Murders of 1940*. The 1940s! The decade all my after-school TV viewing had been preparing me for! It was meant to be. My character was an older aristocrat in her early fifties whom a bunch of young theater hopefuls are trying to impress so she'll give them money to put on a show. The fact that I was ten years younger than the people playing the "young" hopefuls was no problem! This was The Theatah, and I was an *actrice,* up for any challenge! I'd simply bring my years of high school experience putting on old-age makeup to bear, because everyone agrees that drawing all over your face with a white greasepaint pencil to simulate wrinkles looks convincing as hell.

My character sits in a chair near the end of Act One while the young hopefuls keep trying to impress her with increasingly frantic and ambitious musical numbers. What they don't know, but the audience sees, is that during one of their numbers Marjorie is stabbed through the back of the chair (hahaha?) by a mysterious villain. So while the perform-

ers think Marjorie isn't responding to their audition because she's not impressed, in reality she's not responding because she's not alive. The crowd dissolves into giggles (supposedly). The trick of this entire gag is that Marjorie, although dead, keeps her eyes open. That's why the audition kids go on singing and dancing for so long. Hilarious!

There was only one problem. Well, actually, there were at least three problems: that I was playing thirty-five years older than I was, that I'd apparently learned nothing from the previous summer's Snak-Ens diet, and that, too late in the rehearsal process, I discovered that one of my special skills was *not* an ability to keep my eyes open for as long as was required. I don't know how the person in the original cast did it. After twenty seconds, my eyes started to water, and after about forty-five seconds, no matter how hard I tried not to, I had to blink. I think we can all agree that in general, dead people don't blink very much. The audience was supposed to laugh at the enthusiasm of the young hopefuls' frenzied auditioning, but on opening night, the biggest laughs came from my supposedly dead Marjorie having dry contact lenses.

In the first professional review I ever received, the *Kalamazoo Gazette* said that while my character died at the end of the first act, they wished—for my sake—that I'd died sooner. (AHAHAHAHAHA—more tears behind the theater.) "Look at it this way," the director said later. "Your reviews can only get better from here."

But I'd never know, because I haven't read a review of myself since that day. I've also never Googled myself. What good can come of it? I've learned over the years that when someone says something really nice about you, in print or otherwise, it has a way of reaching you. Friends and agents can't wait to tell you when someone says something positive. When the papers say something not so nice, your friends (and agents) get a shifty faraway look, or say nothing, and that tells me everything. What more details would I possibly need— "I wish she'd died sooner"?

In high school, my acting teacher, Brian Nelson, told us there were only two important pieces of feedback in the theater: if someone told you they liked what you did, or if they said they couldn't hear you well enough. As an actor, "speak up" is a pretty objectively helpful piece of criticism. The rest is just one person's opinion. (Though the one thing I'd add is "pronounce words correctly." And try to know the difference between a stringed instrument and a fish.)

Years later, I would finally make it to BroadWAY after all, and it was just as thrilling and exhilarating as I'd imagined— quite literally a dream come true. But my name was on the poster, and I discovered there was a lot of pressure and responsibility that came with that. And even though I was honored to play Miss Adelaide in the revival of *Guys and Dolls* and loved being a member of that incredible company, a part of me also longed for simpler days, back when it was plenty thrilling to just be in the chorus of *Oklahoma!* and *Brigadoon*, when the furthest my imagination could stretch—the biggest success I dared wish for, the closest I thought I'd ever get to the dream of becoming like my idols from *The 4:30 Movie*— was to have my picture hanging in the lobby of a small theater in Augusta, Michigan.

Lauren Graham

You Can't Be Vegan
Just for Ellen

. . . .

I worry about this chapter because I'm pretty sure it's the only one I'll get asked about when I'm promoting this book on the *Today* show. (Hi, Matt!) No matter what else public figures accomplish, we just seem to want to know what they eat for breakfast and what their beauty routine is. Next up: Ruth Bader Ginsburg on being a Supreme Court justice, and how she successfully tackles a bad hair day! You at home can be the *judge*! In our next segment, President Hillary Clinton (it's only March as I write this, so I'm just guessing) shares her State of the Union highlights and her red-carpet slim-down secrets!

I wish we could all stop worrying about it so much, but that's probably unrealistic. So, rather than tell you not to worry, I'm going to tell you some of the Top-Secret Hollywood Secrets I've learned, and save you a ton of money instead!

Here's one: diet books are worthless. Don't spend one penny more on them. Not one more. I'm serious. They all tell you a version of the exact same thing: eat less, work out more.

Now, I'm not a doctor, and I'll probably never play one on TV, because can you imagine? During the original series, *Gilmore Girls* table reads were held in the same conference room where the crime procedural *Cold Case* had theirs, and sometimes I'd pick up one of those scripts and try to read the lines out loud with a straight face—not making fun of them, but really trying to sound convincing. Anyone who happened to be in the room would inevitably fall down on the floor holding their stomach and laughing. The lines weren't bad; I was.

The problem is, I'm physically incapable of sounding at all convincing as a police-type person or a private investigator. In fact, I'm not even sure that the job of the character on *Cold Case* was either of those things, because while all those jobs are of course distinct and challenging and incredibly impressive in real life, on TV I find they all blend together, and all I hear is "I'm extremely sincere and competent." As an actor person, as well as a person person, I don't think I naturally exude competence. I exude more of an "I'm kind of winging it here, but isn't this fun?" type of a vibe. Which is probably not what you'd want coming from the person driving your ambulance. Or a doctor. Or Dexter.

Speaking of fake doctors, my sister worked for a literary agent for a while, which is how I learned the interesting fact that early drafts of the scripts for doctor-type shows don't have all the technical medical jargon in them yet. While writers of a medical show probably have some sort of general doctor-ish knowledge, there are experts whose specialty it is to make sure the lines are accurate. The writer and the accuracy person don't necessarily work together every day, so an early draft of a script might have the major story beats and the personal juicy character stuff that the writer of the script is in charge of, but instead of medical jargon, there'll be placeholder words. In the case of the medical show my sister told me about, the words, aptly, were "medical, medical." As in "Yes, Dr. Jones, I'd love to meet you in the supply closet, but first I have to administer forty ccs of medical medical to my patient's medical medical or he may go into medical medical, and then we'll *really* be in trouble."

"Medical, medical" immediately became a sort of "yada, yada, yada" for my sister Shade and me. Its origin was as a placeholder for what's to come, but it quickly became an even more general placeholder for us. It could mean anything from "You know what I'm talking about" to "Ugh, why is this purse so expensive?" If my sister was at work and didn't have enough time to tell me about a date she'd gone on, she'd say, "He talked about himself the whole night, his shoes were weird, medical, medical," and I'd know exactly what she meant.

So I'm not even a good *fake* doctor. I'm more comfortable saying "medical medical" than spewing any actual technical jargon, and therefore the extent of my health advice is this: just don't eat a lot of crap, take walks, thank you for buying this book, the end.

But Lauren, you live in Hollywood, where the most incredibly attractive, healthy-looking people are! Can't you give us more insight than that?

Okay, fine. Here are some more of the Top-Secret Hollywood Secrets I've learned from years of talking to the best nutritionists, personal trainers, Eastern and Western medicine practitioners, and famous skinny people. Every bit of advice below was actually given to me by a fancy person, or someone who knows a fancy person and the methods they use to stay fancy.

Over the years, I've been told that meat is an important protein; meat is bad for you; the best way to lose weight is to eat a high-protein diet; the best way to lose weight is to eat a vegan diet; juicing is good for you; juice cleanses are pointless; someone with my blood type should eat only lamb, mutton, turkey, and rabbit, and avoid chicken, beef, ham, and pork; bacon is okay; bacon is bad for you; consuming fat helps you lose weight; all fats should be avoided or used minimally; yogurt helps your digestion; yogurt has no impact on your digestion; calcium from dairy is good for you; dairy is bad for you; gluten is no problem for people without celiac disease; everyone should be gluten-free; kale is a superfood; too much kale can actually result in a thyroid condition causing you to *gain* weight; and using non-natural toothpaste can cause bloating of up to five pounds. Just eating fruits and vegetables? Sure, that sounds like a good plan, as long as you aren't sensitive to nightshades (eggplant, tomatoes, peppers), like some people are. You could probably be fine if you ate nothing but spinach all day, unless it's the spinach that was part of the recent salmonella recall. Fruits are okay, but some fruits, like bananas, are so high in natural sugar you might as well eat a piece of cake. What's that? You're still eating regular, processed sugar, the kind that's actually *in* cake? AHMAGAH, how are you still standing? Should I call an ambulance? If indeed you do end up at the hospital, just remember you shouldn't eat grapefruit before taking medications because it can block their effectiveness. So enjoy your new diet of berries and water, people—unless you're allergic to strawberries, that is, as many people are! And don't forget to also be very very very worried about GMOs! And don't drink just *any* water either: tap water is obviously poison, but beware the BPAs in your bottled water too. Also, try to get the type of bottled water that addresses your imbalanced pH levels, because while you may not know it yet, most of us are too acidic and not alkaline enough! Well, there you have it! Make sense? After all, I've given you the secret to everything. It's obvious what you should do now. Could it be any clearer? You're welcome!

What's that? Huh? My editor, Jennifer E. Smith, has just informed me that my book is late. Wait, no, that can't be, because you're reading it! I got confused, since that's what she's calling me about 99 percent of the time. Oh—it's something else! She thinks the above list may be a little confusing for readers. Um, okaaaay, Jen, my ladies and gents are pretty sharp, and I'm fairly certain it isn't confusing to them, but fine, just in case, I now give you the extremely easy-to-read food/diet chart, which is given out only in Hollywood. DON'T TELL ANYONE I GAVE THIS TO YOU!

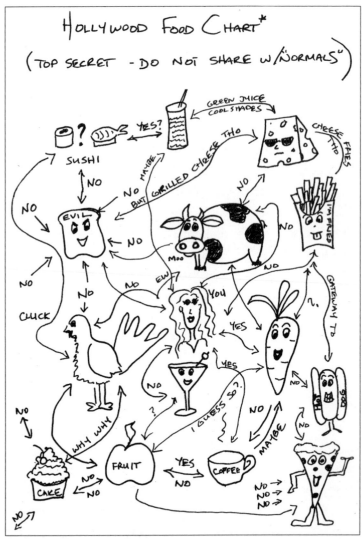

Wow! I cannot believe you guys got me to give you the Top-Secret Hollywood Secrets food chart! I am going to get in so much trouble!

Now, moving on to working out. You may not believe this, but some of the ways regular people stay in shape are actually the same here too! I've been told that non-Hollywood people run or walk outside or on a treadmill, attend classes, and do yoga. Well, we here in Hollywood also do those things. But in Hollywood, clinical trials have shown that you burn more calories if you run while being photographed by paparazzi. Also, spinning classes are proven to be more effective if you spin while being motivated (read "screamed at") by someone who is ten years younger and ten times more attractive than you. Yoga must be done in a studio where the temperature is at least 411 degrees. Oh, and you should probably start working on your ensemble now for the workout class you have in three days. As a person, you are worthless without a high-fashion workout ensemble. These are the only basic differences between Hollywood and you.

Also, I've learned it's not enough to just work out vigorously three to five times a week, because your body is smarter than you are and quickly adapts to any athletic activity you do repeatedly, rendering your efforts almost useless. To combat this, you must constantly change up your already vigorous routine so that you "trick" your body in order to keep it guessing. This sounds strange, I know. In fact, just this morning while I was driving to spin class I was thinking about how odd the concept is, and it occurred to me that BWAHAHA-HAHA, the joke's on YOU, Body, 'cause I was taking your ass to PILATES, ha! See what I did there?

A Japanese healer once told me that because I don't breathe properly, most of the exercise I do does not even register with my physical self. Sometimes you have a body that just won't quit. But in this case, I'm stuck with one that refuses to listen. Hollywood has taught me you must never relax with regard to your body—it is out to get you! You must stay at least one step ahead of your body at all times.

That makes no sense, you say. *How are you supposed to do that?* Guys, it's all in the chart. I mean, come on.

But you all have personal trainers who do all the work for you! It's not fair!

When I can, I work out with Michelle Lovitt, an incredible person who is an excellent trainer and friend. Michelle is positive and knowledgeable and encouraging and also happens to be a super babe. From Michelle, I've learned useful information: you have to be consistent, and it helps to wear a heart rate monitor to keep track of calories burned and make sure you're in the fat-burning zone. Of course, it is enormously helpful to work out with a partner who knows her stuff, but as another trainer I know says: "We aren't the dry cleaner—you can't just do whatever you want during the off-hours and expect to pick up your clothes an hour later looking like new." *You* are the clothes in this scenario—does that make sense? Maybe we need another chart?

I think part of our frustration/fascination in this arena is because we're always holding out hope that there's a secret combination of elements that will make something that isn't easy a little easier: "I started putting lumps of grass-fed butter in my coffee and the pounds just melted away!" But I'm sorry to tell you that, in my experience, there's no secret to accomplishing almost any goal worth pursuing.

And what *is* the goal exactly? To make it to the Smucker's

salute on the *Today* show? (Hi, Natalie!) My grandmother is turning ninety-six years old in a month, and I don't think I've ever seen anything labeled "organic" in her refrigerator. She's a woman of deep faith and intelligence—maybe we should try bottling that? (Someone call *Shark Tank*!)

I know it's frustrating, but don't despair. I have a few more Top-Secret Hollywood Secrets for you.

1. If you're trying to lose weight, you're going to be hungry most of the day, fairly cranky, and irritating to your friends—or maybe it's your friends who are irritating; it's hard to tell because you're so hungry—and you need to be like this every day for about two weeks to see results.

2. I lost the most weight once right after a bad breakup, and then again while rehearsing a Broadway show. Try to arrange for these things to happen at the same time and then you'll really be looking good!

3. Most successful diets involve eating very clean, healthy foods in small quantities, with very few carbohydrates, almost no sugar, very little alcohol, and a ton of physical activity. This combination appears in almost every diet book out there. You can combine foods, count points, or act like you are French, Greek, Spanish, or Beyoncé. While each diet varies slightly, I've read every single one of them and I can assure you they all have the above in common.

4. Bell-bottoms will go in and out of style every few years *for the rest of your life.* This is a bit off topic, but

just another thing I keep meaning to tell you. They'll
change them just enough to make you think you
need new ones. You do not. Keep the ones you already have.

Stars may or may not be just like us, but generally I've
learned it's a mistake to think anyone else has the answer to
pretty much anything. When I hear Kim Kardashian lost her
baby weight on Atkins, I'll eat steak for three days straight
until I remember that, oh yeah, I've tried this before and it
didn't make me feel that great. You have to find what works
for you, not what works for someone else. I kept trying to be
a vegan until I realized that part of my motivation was that I
wanted to be able to go on the *Ellen* show and bond with her
over it. I respect and adore Ellen so much, and she's always
been so supportive of me as an actor, writer, and producer.
Because of her, I got to turn my novel *Someday, Someday,
Maybe* into a pilot script for the CW, and I co-wrote another
half-hour pilot for her company as well. She gave me opportunities I'd never had before, and it's like I wanted to repay her
by being more like her, which, if you think about it, is also the
premise of the stalker movie *Single White Female*. It's great to
look up to people you admire, but you can't make life decisions motivated by the hope that you'll be invited to Ellen
and Portia's to eat lentils and watch *Scandal*.

Anyway, if you're truly fed up and confused about all this,
good news! For you, we have Soylent, a sludge-colored meal
replacement concoction invented by people in Silicon Valley
to enable them to cut out the pesky time that eating requires
(lunch, pah—what a waste of brainpower!) and devote more

time to creating new face-swapping apps. Meals including *food?* What are you, some sort of time-wasting East Coast pizza eater?

Every morning my father eats half a loaf of bread with butter, a giant smoothie, maybe an omelette with cheese, and then he has breakfast. I just want a piece of toast once in a while—is that so wrong?

Plus, I think it should be against the law to feel down on yourself regarding any issues that Oprah is still working on, and OPRAH IS STILL WORKING ON THIS ISSUE. She has rubbed elbows with heads of state and every celebrity in the universe, opened a school in Africa among other accomplishments, made millions of dollars, and helped scores of people live a better life, but, by her own admission, she is still working on diet-related topics. So to sum up: let's all chillax about it and spend more time being kind to ourselves and doing truly useful things like trying to resuscitate words that were never cool, like *chillax*.

Good news! My accountant has just informed me that by imparting all these Top-Secret Hollywood Secrets to you, I've now saved you at least one zillion American dollars! Just make sure to mention me when you talk about it on the *Today* show (Hi, Kathie Lee and Hoda!).

There Is Only One Betty White, or: Paper Towels, a Love Story

· ·

I don't know if we'll ever live in a world where sixteen-year-old boys will throw their PlayStations in the trash because they've discovered they'd rather sit in the movie theater watching *Best Exotic Marigold Hotel 12,* but I'm guessing it probably won't be in my lifetime. Most movies are made for people who want to watch *Jurassic World* over and over. Hollywood is mostly for young people, and young people mostly like to look at other young people because that's who they relate to. The people who pay for movies and TV to get made are mainly making them for young people too. In television, "young people" are people ages eighteen to forty-nine. You may have heard of these people—they're sometimes referred to as the "key demographic." They're the ones whose attention advertisers most want to capture on television and in the movies, and I'm going to tell you why: paper towels.

I was recently at the house of a friend who'd just made

one of those trips to Costco where you feel really smug about all the money you saved until you get home and can't fit the twenty-pound jar of generic peanut butter in any of your cupboards because you forgot about the ten giant jars you already have. So she was trying to get rid of some stuff. She offered me one of those twelve-packs of paper towels that can also be used as an air mattress if you have a guest over, and I was pretty psyched to take it off her hands. I happened to actually need paper towels, and I was like, wow, what a great coincidence. Then I looked at them a little more closely, and I realized they weren't *my* brand of paper towels.

I always feel guilty when I use paper towels, but what makes me feel slightly better is getting the kind that are perforated at narrower intervals and can be ripped off into smaller sections. I feel better because at least I'm not using a whole towel. So I turned down these free, non-perforated paper towels, which my friend thought was crazy, and that's how I suddenly realized I was out of the key demo.

To some degree, I get why our business likes 'em young. Advertisers want people they can convert, people who haven't yet made up their minds about things like what their favorite paper towels are or what car they like to drive—people who might change their minds and switch to a different brand because of the ads they see. But as consumers get older, they decide what they like to use and they hardly ever deviate, which means advertisers need to move on to influence the next batch of potential paper towel devotees. Which is why there aren't more older people—especially women, who apparently have a tendency to pick their paper towel preferences earliest—in movies and television.

"But what about Betty White?" you ask. You're right! Betty White is hilarious, talented, and still working. That is so incredibly rare that she is literally the only person anyone ever mentions when challenging my paper towel theory. No one ever says "What about Betty White and Bathsheba Phlellington?" because Bathsheba Phlellington stopped getting work years ago, and that's only partially because I made her up. There simply isn't a ton of work for women in her category, and therefore there isn't one other example of a Betty White type other than Betty White herself. There are a handful of women who are slightly younger than Betty that I could cite as examples, it's true, but I dare you to name five who aren't Meryl Streep and Diane Keaton or who don't also have the word "Dame" in front of their name.

Carrie Fisher is one of my favorite actors and writers. I've enjoyed her films, seen her on Broadway, and read everything she's written. When I was writing my novel *Someday, Someday, Maybe,* I kept her *Postcards from the Edge* on my desk the whole time, and when I got stuck I'd pick it up and reread sections I'd already read a dozen times. Our books are very different, but the fact that she is an actress who wrote a novel—one that was loosely based on her own life—and became a successful screenwriter was a big inspiration to me.

Recently Carrie Fisher responded to a *New York Post* article that quoted her mentioning the pressure she'd felt to lose weight for the most recent *Star Wars* film. The writer commented that if she didn't like being judged on her looks, she should "quit acting." He went on to say, regarding her work as a writer, "No one would know the name Carrie Fisher if it weren't for her ability to leverage her looks."

Carrie Fisher is a bestselling author and screenwriter, giant movie star, and all-around attractive person. And there are a lot, and I mean a lot, of really beautiful people in New York and Los Angeles who've come to those places in an attempt to become actors. If getting work as an actor was simply about leveraging your looks—if that was the sole currency of success in our field—then everyone on *Vanderpump Rules* would be winning Oscars one day and I would be the center pullout thing in next month's *Maxim*. I'm not saying either thing can't happen, but it hasn't yet, perhaps because there's at least a subtle difference between acting on a reality show and modeling, on one hand, and being a talent like Carrie Fisher, on the other. "Leveraging one's looks" is just one component. Also, I'm not even sure *Maxim* has a center pullout thing.

One day I might not feel like "leveraging my looks" anymore, and I'm okay with that. I'd like to age gracefully, although I'm not yet entirely sure what that will mean. I just know there are certain things I don't want to have to do to look younger. I don't have problems with plastic surgery in theory. Wait—that's not true. I do sort of have problems with it. I'm just trying to sound blasé about something that's currently fashionable but also troubling to me. See also: high-waisted jeans.

For starters, as a viewer, I just can't stand it when it's all I can see. Suddenly I go from watching a scene with two actors I like to being more focused on a conversation between Upper Lip Filler and Botox, and it's too distracting. If I could be guaranteed that no one, including myself, would notice something I did to my face to look younger or somehow better, maybe I'd do it, but I feel like I have one of those faces that shows that sort of stuff too easily, and I don't want to be worried that you'll start mistaking my forehead for a skating rink.

Also, while there's nothing wrong with doing things to make you feel better, I just wish the choices were limited to simpler things many of us have access to, like drinking more water or jogging or finding a more flattering shade of lipstick. It's a bummer that it's even an option to appear more youthful by chopping off your ears and reattaching them in order to hoist up your neck flaps (this may not be the precise surgical term). It's confusing to me that my aversion to doing that has any sort of bearing on my work as an actor. "You mean you aren't willing to chop off and reattatch your ears in order to hoist up your neck flaps, Lauren? Don't you care about us? Where's your commitment to your craft?" mean people on the Internet yell. I wish this possibility simply didn't exist, so that we all had somewhat of a fair playing field. But this is as futile a concept as my belief that everyone who's born should automatically be allowed to live until age eighty-five. The people who treat themselves the most healthfully would get extra credit, more time to live longer; the partiers and couch potatoes would get docked points, living less long. This system is much more fair than the random "sometimes smokers live into their nineties, while marathon runners occasionally drop dead at forty-five" thing we've got going now. But alas.

Another remarkable thing about Betty White is that she went from being twenty- and thirtysomething Betty to eightysomething Betty while maintaining the same wonderful quality she always had of just plain being Betty White.

No matter what character she plays, Betty White is always funny, always smart, and always at least a little sexy. She didn't set herself up early on as hot temptress Betty White, and therefore she didn't have to desperately try to cling to her hot temptress persona, pretending with each passing year that nothing had changed. She didn't have to face headlines like "Betty White: Hot Temptress! Back and Better than Ever!" or "Betty White: Still Hot Temptress?" or "Sad Betty White Seen Clubbing at Limelight! Desperate to Reign as Hot Temptress Once More!" Also, that Limelight (which closed in the 1990s, I think) is literally the only club name I could think of should tell you a great deal about my clubbing habits.

In *The First Wives Club,* Goldie Hawn's actress character says there are only three ages for women in Hollywood: "babe, district attorney, and *Driving Miss Daisy*." This suggests that acting careers follow a three-act structure, which makes sense. For the people who are willing to do the ear-staple-neck-flap surgery, perhaps the second act lasts longer. I haven't gotten to my last act yet (Ole Granny Sack Pants? Cranky Irish Potato Maven?), but so far for me career-wise, I'd call my first two acts Gal About Town and The Mom.

Gal About Town is a career girl on the go. She's looking for love but can't be tied down yet because she's trying to get ahead at the office. Occasionally she's part of a couple, but mainly she's single and career-focused and goes out on dates that don't go well. GAT meets friends in bars and stays out late and takes fashion risks. She wears high-heeled shoes and her winter coat is red or yellow. She has lots of girlfriends she can call when times get tough. Often one of her best friends is a guy she could never picture herself being with romantically, but eventually she'll realize she was wrong and he was the one all along, and isn't it ironic that he was right there in front of her the whole time? When I started out, I did a lot of guest spots and almost all of them were GATs: *Seinfeld*, *Law & Order*, and *NewsRadio*.

My other Gals About Town:

Liz in *Good Company*
Molly in *Conrad Bloom*
Jules in *One True Thing*
Sue in *Bad Santa* (she *really* got around town)
Maggie in *Because I Said So*

The Mom, on the other hand, wears plaid shirts and sneakers, and is usually described as "tired," "beleaguered," or possessing a "faded beauty." The Mom is often harried or overworked, and we know this because, usually in her very first scene, she says frustratedly: "Guys, c'mon! We're going to be late!" The Mom is often single, but we don't always know exactly why, or what happened. There will be one scene where The Mom is with her kid(s) and wistfully refers to "your father," but we aren't sure if he's dead or just away somewhere. Weirdly, The Mom doesn't seem to have that many friends. At most, she has one recently divorced friend who dates younger men and smokes and tells The Mom she needs to get out more. While the GATs usually have tons of personality traits and quirks, The Moms aren't usually as specific. Almost every Mom I've played has a scene where she folds laundry. The GATs never do this. They must be too busy having dates with Mr. Wrong and getting their dry cleaning delivered. Sometimes members of the crew on a Mom project won't even use my character name but will just refer to me as "The Mom": "Okay, now, The Mom stands over here with the laundry basket." I don't know why The Mom can't be as specific and unique as the GATs. I think it's because the GATs are most often in the center of the story and The Mom seldom is, because, paper towels.

My Moms have included:

Joan in *Evan Almighty*
Phyllis in *Flash of Genius*
Pamela in *Max*
Jules in *Middle School*

By the time I was cast as Sarah Braverman on *Parenthood,* playing the mom of two teenagers was age appropriate. But the first time I read *Gilmore Girls,* I was thirty-one years old. I had played the mother of a brand-new baby once (Denise on *Townies*), but even that character was considered a very young mom. For four years in Los Angeles I'd been almost exclusively in the GAT world. But that was about to change.

When I got the script for the *Gilmore Girls* pilot, I was in New York, staying in a friend's studio apartment, waiting to hear if the series I'd just completed for NBC—Don Roos's *M.Y.O.B.*—was going to be picked up for a second season or cancelled. Waiting to hear if your TV show is going to be picked up or not is always a stressful time. "Did you hear anything?" you ask your agent roughly twelve times a day. By call number five, your agent mysteriously begins to be "in a meeting," "with Hugh Jackman buying pants," or "out foraging for truffles."

The *Gilmore Girls* script had actually been sent to me once before, but I hadn't read it. I didn't want to read something and fall in love with it only to find out I wasn't available. But they hadn't found anyone, and they were still interested. "They'll take you in second position now," my agent told me, which meant that, unlike the first time I'd been sent the script, they were willing to roll the dice. If I auditioned and they wanted me, they'd go ahead and shoot the pilot with me, hoping the other show didn't get picked up.

And that's what happened.

Well, what *really* happened was that I got the part, shot the pilot, and chewed off my fingernails for the next three months, during which time *Gilmore Girls* was picked up at the WB, but *M.Y.O.B.* wasn't yet cancelled at NBC—there was still the possibility of a second season. Years later, one of the TV executives who'd been involved at the time told me they'd finally cleared me for *Gilmore Girls* because they'd "swapped me" for another actor at some other network who was also tied to two projects, confirming my suspicion that if you want to know what Hollywood is really like, just watch *The Hunger Games* over and over.

But after all that, the part was mine, and I was set to play Lorelai Gilmore, the thirty-two-year-old mother of a sixteen-year-old girl. When I told people the premise of *Gilmore Girls,* most of them, especially other actresses my age, would inevitably say, "Don't you worry about getting typecast as The Mom? Aren't you worried it will age you?" But honestly, I never once thought about it. To me, Lorelai was equal parts

Gal About Town and The Mom, plus a magical mix of smarts and humor that made her totally unique. I read somewhere that Christopher Reeve said one of the ways he knew a part was for him was when he couldn't stand the idea of anyone else doing it. I know that exact feeling. There's a sort of manic recognition that happens very rarely when I read something I want so much that I go briefly but totally bonkers. That feeling is a combination of "Hello, old friend" meets EVERYONE GET OUT OF MY WAY SHE'S MINE ALL MINE.

At the time, I'd been in a string of shows that hadn't lasted very long. I worked enough, and fairly steadily, but nothing had come close to sticking. Yet when I told my mom about *Gilmore Girls,* I remember her saying, "I have a feeling about this one."

And she was right.

I know how lucky I am to have had such wonderful first and second acts in my career. I'm still not sure what my third act will turn out to be (Sexy Baking Competition Hostess? Flamboyant Peruvian Bingo Caller?), but if you happen to run into Betty White, tell her thank you.

I'd like to be like her one day.

What It Was Like, Part One

. . . .

Do you ever find yourself walking down the street thinking "I feel like Lauren likes me, but does she *love* me?"

The answer is yes. Yes, I do. And I'm going to prove it to you by doing something I haven't done in approximately fifteen years—not even for friends or relatives or employers.

I'm going to watch myself on television.

I'm not sure when I stopped watching things I was in— it's probably more like I never really started. I learned fairly early on that I was not one of those actors who was helped by seeing myself onscreen. It took at least three viewings of something I was in to even begin to be objective, and on *Gilmore Girls,* we did twenty-two episodes each season. If I stayed inside watching myself for all those hours, I'd never make it out to the grocery store, not to mention I'd become unbearable as a human. Making so many episodes for seven years straight did something funny to my memory too, and so today it's hard to recall exactly what was going on back then, or distinguish season from season. But I want to tell you what it was like for me to play Lorelai all of those years. So I'm going to at least scroll through all the episodes to see what I can come up with, to give you a sense of it as best I can. The Internet has already done its job in terms of ranking episodes and naming its favorites. My goal here is just to give you my take on what was going on personally.

Just so you have a visual: I'm in my apartment in Manhattan, and it's the summertime. It's a million degrees outside, and my sister and most of my friends who live here are out of town at a beach somewhere. There's almost no one in my apartment building. Which means not only am I going to spend the next three days watching myself, I am also going to be my only company. So if, during this time, TMZ reports that I've gone crazy and trapped the Chinese-food delivery man inside my apartment because I "just needed someone to talk to," you'll understand why.

MAKING THE PILOT

Alexis Bledel and I met for the very first time in the lobby of a hotel in Toronto. Can you believe that? We'd both been cast in the show without ever having met. I was cast very late in the process, partially because of the *M.Y.O.B.* thing. So there was no time for a chemistry read—usually a minimum requirement when casting two actors whose relationship is vital to the success of a show. There'd been no time for anyone to even see us standing side by side, just to make sure we looked related. We met in that lobby and went straight to dinner with our new employers, series creator Amy Sherman-Palladino, executive producer Dan Palladino, and producer Gavin Po-lone. I was overwhelmed, but I could tell I liked her right away. She was only eighteen years old, but kind and curious, and beautiful of course. I had a good feeling about us from the start. We clicked as friends right away too. But it was all a stroke of luck!

A few months later, the show was picked up, which was exciting but also worrisome, because, as mentioned, I wasn't actually available to do it. If NBC decided they wanted to keep going with *M.Y.O.B.*, I'd have to be replaced on *Gilmore Girls*. So, in a strange sort of limbo, I traveled to New York in May 2000 for the upfronts—the annual event where networks present their new season to advertisers—to promote *Gilmore Girls*. In the greenroom, where the actors and executives mingled before going onstage, there was a giant screen where a clip reel of all the new shows being launched was playing on a loop. Some WB executives came over to introduce themselves.

"The show looks great," one of them said, just as my face came on the screen behind him.

"Tough time slot," said another.

"Why, what's the time slot?" I asked.

Today, if a new show of mine was picked up, that's one of the first things I'd want to know. Back then, it somehow hadn't occurred to me to find out.

"Thursdays at eight," he told me.

Even the less savvy me of the time knew what that meant.

My stomach dropped. "Oh, so we're already cancelled," I joked. He didn't say anything, but smiled sympathetically and sort of shrugged in a way that said he didn't disagree.

Thursday night on NBC was, in the year 2000, the biggest ratings night on all of television. We'd be up against *Friends,* the number one show at the time. The WB itself was still very new, and the ratings, even of their most successful shows, already tended to be much lower than those of the big four networks. So on Thursday nights against America's favorite sitcom, we had almost zero chance of finding an audience.

Oh, well, I thought, I probably can't do this show anyway. And even if I was let out of my *M.Y.O.B.* contract, I faced a Thursday time slot that basically spelled doom. Here we go again, I thought. I'd worked fairly steadily since moving to Los Angeles from New York, but every single show I'd done up until then had been cancelled in its first season. Why should *Gilmore Girls* be any different? I'd fallen in love with the script right away, but I loved *M.Y.O.B.* too, and the ratings were only so-so. My show business heart had been broken before, and I was starting to get used to it.

I turned back to the clip reel just as *Gilmore Girls* came on again. Goodbye, new show! I said to myself.

In front of me, two women who looked to be pretty close in age were watching the screen. As our scenes played, they gasped and grabbed onto each other, their faces lighting up. "Mom, that's us!" the daughter said, beaming at her young-looking mother. They seemed shocked and pleased to see themselves reflected in the characters. Something had clearly struck a chord with them in a big way.

Hmmmm.

SEASON ONE

The first scene we filmed is the first scene you see in the pilot: a guy in Luke's hits on Rory, and then Lorelai, and we reveal they aren't girlfriends, as he assumed, but in fact mother and daughter. Watch it back and you won't believe you're watching a young actress (Alexis) in her first on-camera scene. Also, what's so funny about this pilot by today's standards is that while the dialogue is delightful from the start, nothing really happens for the first fifteen or twenty minutes, until Rory gets into Chilton and Lorelai has to ask her parents for money. Today, if a mother and daughter speaking clever dialogue didn't also reveal themselves to be surgeons, werewolves, or undercover detectives by the end of the teaser, we'd never be picked up. Also, we all look twelve years old.

Frankly, what I remember most when I watch this season is the degree to which I was on an adrenaline-fueled dialogue high the whole year, if that makes any sense. I hadn't had material this dense since back in acting school. I found the pace and sheer volume of it exhilarating. Rather than being tired out by the long hours, I had extra energy as a result. I slept about four hours a night and still felt great. I ran every day at lunch in the WB gym. Ah, youth!

Watching Scott Patterson this season reminds me—you know, that part wasn't necessarily the inevitable love interest for Lorelai that it became. He was simply Cute Grouchy Diner Owner in the beginning, and it could have gone in any number of directions, but Luke took on a more important role because of Scott's special sexiness, which was mixed with a gruffness that was the perfect contrast to Lorelai's chirpy cheerfulness. Watch and learn, young actors—if you're interesting, the camera finds you.

Kelly Bishop and Ed Herrmann were perfectly cast as Emily and Richard. They both exude aristocratic elegance that tells you right away the kind of household Lorelai grew up in, and why she might have found it a bit stuffy at times. As actors, they both have emotional depth and impeccable comic timing. Plus, as people, they're pure joy to be around.

A few months into filming that year, I remember Alexis and I went to see Melissa McCarthy perform in the Groundlings for the first time, and we were completely blown away by her. I wondered then if anyone would ever figure out a way to expose how uniquely talented she was. Of course her Sookie character was a delight, but could she find a way to showcase the other hilarious and original characters she was able to create? Why yes, People. Yes, she could.

David Sutcliffe's Christopher is so appealing it makes you wonder once in a while if Lorelai and Rory's dad should have stayed together after all. And Yanic Truesdale created such a unique character in Michel, especially since, in person, he's warm and funny and hardly ever suffers from ennui like Michel does.

So many other special players make Stars Hollow what it is: I'm always wowed by Sally Struther's humor and warmth, Liz Torres's sultry delivery, and Sean Gunn's total commitment to whatever Kirk's new passion is. I love the fun feuds between Lane and Mrs. Kim, Michael Winters makes those long Taylor speeches look effortless, and Rose Abdoo's Gypsy is just a gem. Most other shows on the WB at the time were peopled with young hotties. I love that we were peopled with a lot of interesting people.

Times were different: Lorelai complains when Emily tries to install a DSL line, claiming she doesn't need one. AHAHAHA, yes, you do, Lorelai, and just you wait a few years till your BlackBerry stops working altogether. Rory wonders if there's still hope for Sean Penn and Madonna (there isn't!); Kelly complains about kids today wasting their time watching "MTV and a hundred TV channels," which doesn't seem like all that many by today's standards; and I write my number down for Max Medina on a business card!

Fashion and hair: Wow, lots of leather blazers and *blue* eye shadow? For some reason, I was very into blue eye shadow this year. My makeup artist at the time worried it was a bit much, but I liked anything bright and bold for Lorelai. Donna Karan nylons abound. They were new and very popular; there were no Spanx back then, and these stockings, with serious control top built in, were revolutionizing ladies' stomachs all across the land. My skirts are very short this year and my hair is veeeeery black and I remember there was much discussion about what to do about it. (The hair, not the skirts. No one in the history of television has ever worried about skirts being too short.) Boring but important hair note: The color was just one of my hair issues. My hair is also naturally curly and extremely sensitive to the weather. This means that in order for me to wear it curly, it has to first be straightened, then curled, which sort of defeats the whole supposed "luck" of having naturally curly hair in the first place. So figuring out how best to make it last throughout a fourteen-hour day took some experimentation over the years. Stay tuned for the exciting results!

What I love: There are so many great episodes from this year, but for me, the show really hits its stride in episode six, "Rory's Two Birthdays," where the Gilmores have a very fancy party for Rory that's in stark contrast to the cozy one Lorelai throws, full of junk food and a cake with Rory's face on it and Stars Hollow locals. Kelly is marvelous in the scene in Lorelai's bedroom where she sees a picture of Lorelai with a broken leg and they both really begin to get, in a new way, how much they've missed not being part of each other's lives. From the start of the show, Kelly named herself my TVM, or TV mom, by which she meant she was taking her character's role seriously, beyond the pages or the sets and out into the real world. Right away we developed the easy rituals of old friends: meeting for lunch at Joe Allen in New York, or out for guacamole at our favorite Mexican place in L.A., or allowing ourselves to split a little bag of Cheetos when we were filming in the middle of the night. In a maternal, protective way, she found most of my boyfriends at the time lacking, and once told me I needed someone who was more my equal, like "that wonderful actor on *Six Feet Under*."

Hmmmm.

Season finale: Over the course of this first season, we began to realize that our tough time slot might actually have been a gift. What expectation could the network possibly have for us to get any ratings against such tough competition? Yet bit by bit, we began to accumulate nice notices and loyal viewers.

In the last episode, Rory finally says "I love you" to Dean, and Max Medina proposes to Lorelai with a thousand yellow daisies. (Although, weirdly, he does it over the phone.) If you've ever seen series creator Amy Sherman-Palladino in person or read her interviews, you already know she's very, very funny, and very, very bright. But the mind of the person who conceives of such a grand romantic gesture as this? Genius.

SEASON TWO

This year the WB moved us to Tuesday nights at eight (so long, *Friends*!), and the ratings began ticking up. I was nominated for a Golden Globe and a SAG Award, and I also got to present at the Emmys. My dates to these events were, in order, my manager, my dad, and my cousin Tim. I was very popular! (With people I worked with and/or was related to.)

Times were different: Christopher gives Lorelai a DVD of *The Graduate* (no Netflix then) and *a disposable camera* (these were a HUGE innovation at the time) to take pictures at Rory's graduation. A classmate of Lorelai's complains about her job at Kinko's (ubiquitous copy places before FedEx took over the world). And Lorelai and Rory invite Dean over to watch the TV movie *Tears and Laughter: The Joan and Melissa Rivers Story,* starring Joan and Melissa Rivers as themselves. (Which reminds me: Joan Rivers was a fellow Barnard alum, and was always so nice and supportive when I saw her on the red carpet. To my knowledge, she always went easy on me, fashion-wise. When I co-wrote a pilot about an aspiring late night talk show host, played by me, I had my character (me) speak to a photo of Joan she keeps on her dressing room mirror. As both a comedian and an inspiration, she is missed.)

Fashion and hair: I mean, I open the season wearing a sleeveless T-shirt with the face of a pug on it. In the second episode, just for variety, I sport a sleeveless T-shirt that gives the illusion that I was also wearing a bunch of pearl necklaces—my fashion evolution this year couldn't be more evident.

Slip dresses were also very big in 2001, and I wear a lot of them this season. Although am I the only one who's noticed that slip dresses are basically indistinguishable from plain old slips because they are, in fact, not dresses but just slips? We were all running around in our undergarments feeling fancy-free. They're back in fashion now, and still no one has blown the lid off this conspiracy to get us to pay more just to wear our underwear in public.

Over the summer I dyed my hair red because it seemed like a fun idea, and then had to dye it back for the show. So this season my hair is black with red undertones, and super-damaged. At some point I did this Japanese straightening treatment that was all the rage then, and my hair turned stick straight and shiny, yet rigid and broom-like.

What I love: Episode 4, "Road Trip to Harvard," where, in the face of Max and Lorelai's breakup, Rory and Lorelai bond on the road, and Episode 7, "Like Mother Like Daughter," where Kelly and I model the same fashions. Also, that diet Michel talks about, where he's reducing his calories by 30 percent because a study showed it helped rats live longer? It was based on the real-life diet of our producer and health buff Gavin Polone. He is to this day extremely thin, although probably also 30 percent hungrier than the rest of us are.

Season finale: Where "Oy with the poodles already" was born! I've said it on command for you in airports across the land, but honestly I forgot where exactly in the show it appeared. Now I remember!

For you speed nerds, note how over the course of this year, the pace of the show increased exponentially, and everyone began talking a whole lot faster. This was around the time when we started to be known for that. Watch the first and last episodes back-to-back, and it's super-evident. I was sort of talking that way already, but it starts to become Stars Hollow–wide. This resulted in our already lengthy scripts getting even longer. Also, I remember having an audition this year and being asked before I went in if I could "talk normally." Ha!

Also, in general, how great is Liza Weil as Paris? Discuss.

SEASON THREE

Ah yes. Here's the episode "Eight o'Clock at the Oasis," where I single-handedly launched Jon Hamm's career by casting him as Peyton Sanders. Just kidding—I had nothing to do with his casting or any of his success to come. But I do remember thinking what a talented, foxy dude he was.

In the episode "Lorelai Out of Water" my fishing-gear looks are truly upsetting, that's my friend Billy Burke playing my beau, and Adam Brody is so charming as Dave Rygalski.

Times were different: In the second episode this year, someone ★69s our cassette-tape-based answering machine!

Fashion and hair: In the opening scene this season, I'm wearing a nightgown—*or is it a slip dress?* Lots of floral prints this year. And it looks like I was giving curly hair another go. Let's see how many episodes I last before abandoning this folly—will I never learn?

What I love: The speech in the first episode where Lorelai confesses to Luke she's worried she'll never have "the whole package" now that she and Christopher have broken up. It was timely for Lorelai, and I think for me too. Amy wrote and directed this episode, and Luke consoles Lorelai in such a generous way, even though you can tell it's causing him pain to do so. Well played, Scott Patterson. And in the episode "The Big One," Liza gives her fantastic "I'm not going to Harvard" speech. Amy wrote this one too. She really is the master of moments that are heartbreakingly funny.

Season finale: That's my sister Maggie sitting right between Rory and Paris at the Chilton graduation.

Over the years, many family members made cameos, in fact. My cousin Tim still talks about his favorite episode: "The one about the guy carrying flowers through the lobby of the Dragonfly." He (obviously) starred in it as The Guy. I'm sure it's your favorite episode too.

Rory's speech to Lorelai at graduation gets me every time. Oh, and the season began with Lorelai having a dream about being with Luke, and ends with Luke having one about Lorelai. I never noticed that parallel before!

SEASON FOUR

In the second episode this year, that's our dialogue coach, George Bell, playing Professor Bell at Yale. One of my favorite pieces of dialogue actually happens a few episodes later, in this exchange between Kelly and me regarding my logo sweatpants:

> EMILY: You have the word "juicy" on your rear end.
> LORELAI: Well, if I'd known you were coming over, I
>   would have changed.
> EMILY: To what—a brassiere with the word "tasty"
>   on it?

Getting my makeup done for "The Festival of Living Art" episode every day for a week taught me that I would never want to be in an actual Festival of Living Art. Torture. However, our makeup artists won an Emmy for this episode, which was pretty darn cool.

Times were different: Rory realizes she wrote her Yale moving-in date down wrong when she double-checks her *Filofax day planner.*

Fashion and hair: The season opens with Lorelai and Rory returning from their backpacking trip through Europe. I'm proud yet horrified to tell you that the entire outfit I'm wearing in the first scene—the kelly-green EVERYONE LOVES AN IRISH GIRL T-shirt, the Ireland soccer jacket, and the oversized knit pom-pom hat with the word DUBLIN on it—were all from my personal closet. Oh, and the gold clover necklace was mine too. I was really hitting the Irish thing hard.

Not sure what I did to my hair in Episode 15, "Scenes from a Mall," but it's suddenly Grand Ole Opry–level voluminous.

What I love: This was a great season for hunky Milo Ventimiglia as Jess facing off against hunky Jared Padalecki as Dean. They are both so talented and equally compelling as suitors, I can see why "teams" formed. I love Michel's devotion to his chow-chow too. This was probably the year Amy and Dan got theirs, to whom they were also extremely dedicated. I also love little clever things, like Rory waking up with a Post-it on her head that Lorelai left as a reminder, and that a tipping point in Lorelai's feelings for Luke is the discovery that "Luke can waltz," embellished with lots of eyebrow wagging on my part, for emphasis.

Season finale: In general, I remember being worried about what would change when Rory went off to college and Lorelai and Rory didn't live together anymore, but I think it was handled well. By the end of this season, Luke and Lorelai (finally) kiss, and Dean and Rory reunite, although he's still married, which is the start of trouble between mother and daughter. All our guys are at bonkers hotness levels this season. And it was so much fun to have my New York–based friend Chris Eigeman, who played Jason Stiles, in town for a while.

SEASON FIVE

This is basically a whole season of Rory and Lorelai having tension, Emily and Richard having tension, and Dean and Lindsay having tension. Fight, fight, fight!

Times were different: Lorelai says something about being worried there's anthrax on her bagel. Anthrax was terrifying at the time, but it seems like a relatively mellow threat given what we face now. Can you imagine being all that worried today about something coming toward you at the speed of the post office? Also, at a Friday night dinner gone wrong, Lorelai asks one of Emily's maids for a *phone book* so she and Rory can order a pizza.

Fashion and hair: Shrugs—little mini-sweaters—are very big this year. Also, wearing short-sleeved shirts layered over contrasting colored long-sleeved shirts. Thankfully, I seem to have managed to tame my country singer hair a bit. I'm wearing my own glasses in "We Got Us a Pippi Virgin," which makes me look a little like Tina Fey, I think. Here I am doing "Weekend Update":

What I love: Talented Matt Czuchry joins the cast, further complicating whom you'd choose as Rory's Destiny. And we hit one hundred episodes this year, which was quite a milestone. To celebrate, they brought the cast and crew down to one of the stages, where we took a big group photo and were given a giant cake to share. At the time I thought this was sort of anticlimactic. Like, "Thanks for the hundreds of hours of work; please enjoy this vanilla icing!" Later I learned that a one-hundred-episode cake is the standard tradition. Every show that gets there does it. We got a cake on *Parenthood* too. So it's a nice thing. But if I ever get close to hitting a hundred episodes again, I'm going to try to bump this tradition up to diamonds, or a chocolate fountain at least.

In our one hundredth episode, Emily and Richard renew their wedding vows. Ed's face as Kelly walks toward him down the aisle is just beautiful.

Season finale: Rory tells Lorelai she wants to take time off from Yale. Lorelai is upset and doesn't want her to move back home. Luke tries to help Lorelai, and her response is "Luke, will you marry me?" And before he even has time to answer her, it's *the end*. Wow. As season finales go, that's a pretty exciting one.

SEASON SIX

While I totally understood the need to keep the story moving in different directions, I have to admit I struggled with the Lorelai/Rory separation this year. It went on for a while, and Lorelai was so crabby with Rory for several episodes, not to mention that I missed my favorite scene partner. I'd never played a character for this long, and while it's a bad actor cliché to say "my character would never do that," the line between personal and professional starts to get so blurry, and after a while you start to feel like what's happening to your character is sort of also happening to you. I remember talking about it with Amy, who felt it was important developmentally that this always-close relationship hit a significant growing pain. Still, I felt bad in scenes where I kept holding a grudge.

Also during this season, Lorelai adopts Paul Anka (the dog, not the person), and Rory and Logan in love are extremely fun to watch!

Times were different: Lorelai attempts to clean house but refuses to part with most of her VHS-tape recordings of old television episodes like *Knots Landing* and *21 Jump Street,* partially "because the commercials are the best part."

Fashion and hair: All my blazers look too short—either that was the fashion that year or I had a growth spurt. Oh, and puffy sleeves on everything—an adornment that my already broad shoulders don't really need. I also seem to be experimenting with wacky necklaces, and wow, my devotion to Diane Von Furstenberg wrap dresses really kicks into high gear this season. The same designer plays an important role in the reboot too, but in an unexpected way . . . wait and see!

What I love: I love the scene with Kelly in the private plane where she blames herself for Rory's troubles. Vulnerable Emily is so compelling, especially because Kelly only lets her out once in a while.

The best part of this season: Episode 9, "The Prodigal Daughter Returns," where Lorelai and Rory reunite! On the lawn outside Lorelai's house, Lorelai tells Rory she looks so much more "silver" than she remembers. I just love little poetic touches like that. And that reunion hug was for real! We were both excited to get back to happier times.

Season finale: In Episode 22, "Partings," Lorelai has a recurring dream of being smothered by a walrus, and gets a therapy session in her car over her hesitation about marrying Luke. (Side note: Will someone please write a thesis paper on all the bizarre dreams these characters have? I still need help deciphering them.) Logan says "I love you," then leaves for London. Luke doesn't like ultimatums, and Lorelai ends up in bed with Christopher. This has all the earmarks of a classic, juicy wacky season finale that tees up the next season wonderfully. But "partings," indeed—I didn't know it then, but this was Amy and Dan's last episode . . . until eight years later.

SEASON SEVEN

Well, in many ways, this was a tough year and sort of a jumble for me, memory-wise. For example, apparently during this season Christopher and Lorelai get married in Paris. Okay. I have to admit, this seemed so odd to me back then (especially after all that time apart; I just didn't think Lorelai would get married without Rory present), that I somehow managed to *completely forget it ever happened.* While we were filming the reboot, Dan Palladino had to call one of the superfan assistants in the office to have her explain the whole episode to me in detail. Even then, I wasn't sure she was telling me the truth: "No. Really? Are you sure? No. *Paris?*" I kept saying to her.

Plus, our network, the WB, merged with another network, UPN, to form a new network, the CW. Like any company, changes at the top trickle down to its employees. The good news was that we survived the merger when many other shows did not. The bad news was that Amy and Dan faced a tough renegotiation and ultimately couldn't agree to terms. Our new show runners were talented writers who knew the show well. But just like when David Lee Roth was replaced as the lead singer of Van Halen, no matter how hard we tried singing the same songs, they just didn't sound quite the same. (Apparently, I stopped listening to music in the 1980s.)

Alexis and I were at the end of our contracts as well, and about halfway through this season we started renegotiating too. It was a confusing time. For starters, after almost seven straight years of extremely long hours, we were both just plain tired. Creatively, we weren't sure where the show was heading, and we were starting to feel a bit uninspired. To both of us, Rory graduating from Yale actually seemed like a logical place to end the story. We both stood to get a raise if we stayed longer, but we loved the show far too much to keep going for that reason alone if the content wasn't good enough. So conversations with our representatives went back and forth, and nothing had been decided by the last day of work. Our director, Lee Shallat Chemel, worried about how best to handle the episode, given that none of us knew if we were filming the last one or not. Ultimately, she decided to mimic the final crane shot from the pilot, where the camera pulls back over Lorelai and Rory talking at their table at Luke's diner. I think she did a fantastic job this season in general, and with that episode specifically. She didn't want to jump the gun, but she also wanted to give the fans some closure in case this was indeed farewell. That last day stretched into the night and ended up being more than twenty-one hours long. I said a bleary and brief goodbye to everyone as the sun was coming up, but it wasn't the quality send-off any of us would have given if we'd known this was the end.

Over the next few weeks, various scenarios were discussed: returning for a full season or possibly a shorter farewell season of just thirteen episodes, trying to entice Amy and Dan to return, or letting the show go altogether. In the midst of these discussions, I was out to dinner with a friend, and right after we ordered, the waiter came back over to our table. "Your agent's on the phone," he told me. He led me over to the bar and handed me the receiver.

"The show's over," my agent said. And suddenly, before the appetizers had even arrived, that was that.

Just like I'd never been on a long-running show before, I'd never been at the end of one either, and I didn't know what the protocol was. That day, I was told that I was the first to know, and was asked to wait before reaching out to anyone. I assumed this meant everyone would be getting a call, and given the size of the cast, they needed time to do that. But I found out much later that Alexis and I were the only cast members who were officially informed, and others found out in far less conventional ways. Ed Herrmann learned the show was cancelled from the clerk at his video store in Connecticut, for example. If I had it to do over again, I'd have called everyone myself, and thrown a party too. To end so abruptly was such an odd conclusion to our epic adventure. Over the next eight years I saw members of the cast socially, but it wasn't until the reunion at the ATX Festival in Austin in March 2015 that we'd all (well, almost all) be together again.

In retrospect, the incomplete feeling that was so unsettling at the time the show ended turned out to be a blessing. Had the story lines been sewn up more neatly, it would have been harder to justify returning to them. Over the years, fans continued to ask about a movie, for good reason—in some ways, the characters had been left frozen in midair, with many questions unanswered. Of course, I too wished we'd had more closure on such an important chapter of my life. But I never could have imagined how incredibly satisfying it would be to come back to it all these years later. I never could have predicted the invention of streaming, the appetite for reboots, and how much *your* enthusiasm would contribute to bringing us back again. I'm thrilled it happened the way it did, but I never saw it coming. You might say I lacked vision, and you'd be right. Frankly, I'm still pretty excited about the whole disposable-camera thing.

Well, I made it through all seven seasons. I did almost take the polite FreshDirect man hostage, but he made it out alive. It was actually nice to revisit the show after all this time. As for the reboot? Well, by my calculations I should be able to watch it sometime in the year 2032. It was so big and wonderful and important to me. The pressure is just too much!

I mean, like I said, I really love you. But for me to watch myself in even *more* episodes? Perhaps, as Richard and Emily did, we'll just have to renew our vows.

Before My REI Card

. . . .

Some Thoughts on Being Single

In 2002, I was paired up with Peter Krause to present at the SAG Awards. We'd met before in the late nineties, on an episode of *Caroline and the City* where we were both guest stars, but back then there was never a hint of anything romantic. I'd followed his career on television as a fan of the too short-lived Aaron Sorkin series *Sports Night,* and been wowed by his work on the incredible HBO show *Six Feet Under.* Our paths crossed occasionally at an event or party, but I avoided handsome actor-types as a rule. Over the years I'd learn that my concerns were unfounded and there was nothing to fear: attractive, straight, successful actors actually don't get as much attention as you might think, because women find them so intimidating that they—AHAHAHAHA, I can't even finish that sentence with a straight face. Those dudes get all the attention you think they do, and then some. So I was generally wary of what I deemed his "type." But we were always friendly. Backstage that night, we made small talk, and just as our names were being announced he turned to me and said calmly: "Want to hold hands?"

It was such an odd, old-fashioned, unexpected question. Did he mean anything by it? If we did walk out holding hands, would people think we were together? Would holding hands make it easier to walk in my very high heels? I hadn't held hands with anyone in what felt like a million years, so I decided it didn't matter. "Yes," I said, and we did, and then we presented the award, and I went back into the audience to sit back down next to my date for the evening, a gainfully employed lawyer who was also my dad. I didn't see Peter again for years.

After I first moved to L.A., I was in a long relationship with a wonderful guy, but I wasn't yet ready to settle down. After that ended, I contracted a case of man-repellent-itis so severe that it is still being studied by the Mayo Clinic. Or at least that's how it felt.

For a very long time I worked and worked and worked, and then I looked up one day and all my friends were married with children. These married-with-children people were still my friends, but they'd become part of a community I wasn't in, a club I didn't belong to. Socially, their lives had completely changed, and they were busy. Their attention had turned to carpools and birthday parties and school tuition, and I was playing catch-up: "Wait, so we *don't* have game night anymore? You guys, who's free for dinner Saturday? Oh, absolutely no one?"

I looked at these friends and realized: Well, duh, work is gratifying, but it isn't everything, and it's no fun to sleep with at night. It just took me longer to see that, and I didn't have the same urgency they had to get to it, but then one day, just like that, I thought, I get it now. I'd be interested in this other stuff. But I'd missed the time when most people around my age had paired off. It was as if I'd misread the schedule at Penn Station and the trains to Happy Couplehood had all left already, and there I was with nothing to do but sit with the drunk business-men at the bar and nurse a warm beer and wait for the trains to start up again. I waited and waited and waited for those trains.

I attended weddings by myself, went to parties I didn't feel like going to, "just in case," and was escorted to events by my dad, my cousin Tim, and my dear friend Sam. "Who's with you tonight? Aww, your dad again?" journalists would say, with a sympathetic frowny face. The only bright spot, dude-wise, was at an event where I met Matthew Perry. He became my longtime Friend Who I Almost But Never Ex-actly Dated, or FWIABNED. We probably all have at least one FWIABNED in our lives. My FWIABNED is very spe-cial to me.

At one point during this time my father was on a plane and noticed a woman reading a magazine I was in. "That's my daughter," he said proudly. The woman turned to him with a look of pity. "Please tell her I didn't meet my husband until late in life—*there's still time,*" she said. Strangers were worried about me; that's how long I was single!

There's nothing wrong with being single, unless, it seems, you're an actor getting interviewed a lot. *Gilmore Girls* was at its peak then, and I was getting interviewed a lot. During these years, when the press asked me if I was seeing someone, I'd just say, "I'm dating." Sometimes that was true and sometimes not. Either way, I wasn't in anything secure enough to talk about or expose publicly. But over time, I felt increasingly vulnerable when I had to face these questions. Magazines don't like it when you say too little about your personal life—it makes the pages very hard to fill. If they had their way, every article would be full of sex and gossip, and I couldn't contribute stories about either. Interviewers seemed increasingly frustrated, and interviews became less about what project I was doing and more a thinly veiled reiteration of "Join us today as we try once again to figure out what is wrong with this poor girl who just can't seem to get a date!"

I knew I didn't want to stand on a red carpet and reveal too much, but I was at a loss as to what or how much to say. You may think there's a sort of School of Fame where actors learn how to handle tricky situations, but there isn't. (Someone call *Shark Tank*!) Not for the first time, I wished there was someone to ask, or a *Peanuts*-style Lucy booth with a sign that said THE DOCTOR IS IN. I wasn't looking for a three-month seminar, just a place I could stop into when I needed a quick answer on how to handle problems I hadn't even known existed back when all I dreamed of doing as an actor was performing in the chorus of a regional theater production of *Oklahoma*. How to walk in heels! Don't Google yourself, and other helpful tips! How to talk to *Us Weekly* about your new or nonexistent relationships! Take a pamphlet! Five cents only!

I learned a few things fairly easily. If you plan to be an actor who is regularly interviewed, you need to start thinking now about your favorite drugstore cheap-and-cheerful beauty products (Chapstick, Neutrogena sunblock, any brand of coconut oil), your go-to workout routine (spinning, yoga, walking across the Brooklyn Bridge), your favorite leave-in conditioner (Davines, Oribe, coconut oil), your latest girl crush (I never have an answer for this—let's just say coconut oil), and, if you're presenting at an awards show, which other presenter you're most excited to meet. Be sure to think of someone beforehand, otherwise, even though you're surrounded by dozens of your idols, you will draw a complete blank: "I'm excited to meet, uh, that guy, from that movie, with the people in it . . ."

At a minimum, you'll be asked each of these questions approximately ten thousand times in every interview for the rest of your life. In addition to being asked to reveal intimate details about your love life, you'll also constantly be encouraged to dish about your co-stars, to which there's only one acceptable answer: that you're obviously one big happy family (which you, savvy reader, already knew). Then, after you successfully dodge this question, they'll ask you who's the best kisser you've ever worked with. DON'T ANSWER THIS. It will result in an article stating you've "broken your silence" about how awful it was to kiss everyone else. Finally, you'll be asked about all the pranks everyone supposedly pulls on each other on set all the time. Most films and television shows have very long hours, and no one I know pulls pranks on set, except maybe George Clooney, though I'm pretty sure I read that in a magazine, so who can say for sure? Incidentally, when I was first doing *Gilmore Girls,* I'd run into George on the lot sometimes, and he was always very nice to me and acted like he knew who I was and treated me like I was behaving normally, which was very kind in the face of my babbling and drooling.

However, it wasn't enough to make George say "Amal, schlamal!" or anything like that, and the weird dating years—and my difficulty explaining them—continued. I was once set up with an actor by my assistant, who was friends with the other actor's assistant. The actor wanted to meet me because he saw my (sort-of real) face on a giant billboard on Sunset Boulevard. You know, the way everybody gets asked out! While on location, I had a fun relationship with someone who revealed at the end of the movie that he had a girlfriend back home. Just like how your grandparents met! I shook hands with a cute guy for the first time while presenting him with an award. Backstage, we had charming banter. He asked for my phone number, and then didn't call me for three months. THREE MONTHS. Of course, when he finally called, I told him politely that he'd waited too long and I didn't appreciate being disrespected like that. AHAHAHA-HAHA. NOPE, I went out with him anyway! I wanted to hold out for men with good behavior, but ultimately I gave in to less-good behavior because I was working all the time and wasn't sure when the next chance to meet someone would be. One thing I learned: starting off with very low standards is a surefire way to ensure they'll be met.

Not surprisingly, none of the relationships that started during Billboard Face Awards Show Presenter Time stuck. After all, how many successful, lasting unions do you know that began with the words "And the winner is . . ."? Plus, if you're meeting someone for the first time after three hours of hair, makeup, and styling, you've already set the bar too high. There is no way they won't be disappointed when you reveal your true self. "Hey, where were those boobs I was promised when I saw you up on the podium?" "They're, um—hey, look over there! Isn't that Ryan Seacrest?" Also, if you think actors are already self-obsessed, imagine actors who are at a show that exists solely to affirm they are indeed as great as they might think they are. Lots of attention and praise and hot girls everywhere bring out the humble side in everyone!

It wasn't just the guys I met who were the problem. In more ways than just being covered in eighty layers of self-tanner, the person they were meeting wasn't really me either. You know how before a party you clean up your house so that everyone thinks you live that way all the time? That's meeting someone at an awards show. It's a way more exaggerated version of meeting anyone you hope to impress for the first time. You present the fresh-flowers-on-the-table, bed-always-made side of yourself first. But ultimately you're going to slip and show your house the way it is on a morning when you're running late for work, or can't find an outfit, and that's a relationship. Ultimately, everyone who gets close to you is going to see inside your closet on its worst day, and their reaction to that is what will tell you if you're going to make it or not. You can't live an entire life secured in by Spanx.

When I started working with Peter on *Parenthood,* he made a lot of references to the fact that we were playing brother and sister. While true that our characters were siblings, I wasn't sure why it kept coming up. He'd hand me a prop or a cup of coffee and then sort of narrate: "I'm handing my *sister* a cup of coffee. That's my *sister* drinking the coffee over there." By week two of work, I wanted to say, "I get it, I get it—you're not interested in me *that way.* Well, I don't trust handsome actors, either, so we're good!" In fact, I think he was actually trying to talk himself out of starting anything. At our age, we'd probably both been through "showmances" that went south and made work an uncomfortable place to be. But ultimately, our mutual wariness gave way without much discussion or effort—it just sort of happened. That's one thing I've learned when it comes to relationships. There's so much to negotiate once you *really* get to know someone— the beginning should feel easy and inevitable.

By the time Peter and I actually started dating seriously, I finally knew exactly how to handle myself and all my public-vs.-private issues instantly melted away. Wrong! Instead of making the public part of life easier, it was even more difficult. Now I actually had someone I cared about, which made me care even more about protecting that person and our privacy and our brand-new status. So I stuck to my old reliable "I'm dating," without naming any names, until journalists started rolling their eyes to my face. This standoff lasted for a while, but eventually more people found out, and I kept getting asked to talk about it. I continued to say no, until I was told an outlet was going to "run with it anyway." What to do? I was going on the *Today* show around then (hi, Savannah!) and was asked if I wanted to "announce" us as a couple. Did I? All I knew for sure was that I felt strange. I went on *Ellen,* where she showed a picture of Peter and me, and I admitted that yes, I was seeing someone, but in a panic I referred to him as "Fred." She had just shown *a picture of me and Peter,* which I had okayed, but somehow in the moment it felt too personal to also say his actual name. Ellen looked at me like I was in-sane, which thankfully I was used to, since that's pretty much our regular relationship. I was confused. She was confused. Lucy, I need more pamphlets!

Not saying anything wasn't really working, but making an "announcement" of any kind just felt so wrong—too big and weird. Today, in order to grab your already taxed attention, news of any kind sometimes gets positioned as an urgent proclamation or a major confession—some massive secret being revealed, rather than what it really is: *Today, an actor you might know from a TV show you may have seen reluctantly admits to something that may or may not be of mild interest to you.*

A few months into dating, Peter and I planned a vacation to go skiing. In preparation, he took me to REI. I had never been to an REI store and didn't know what REI stood for or what they sold there. I asked him why we had to go. He asked me where I thought people went to get outdoor gear, and I was like, "Um, not Barney's?" No, Lauren, not Barney's. What I was to discover at REI would blow my mind—and, weirdly, help me understand show business better.

First of all, the sign on the front door says FREE WI-FI AND INSPIRATION. Whoa. I was impressed by this offer, which was already better than some nice hotels I've stayed in. In fact, if you go to REI right now, you'll probably find me in the glamping section checking my email and eating freeze-dried watermelon!

It didn't take me long to realize that everyone who works at REI is named Tad. Tad has zero percent body fat and a deep tan. From the joyous way Tad describes the absorbency levels of the Shammie Wowzas by the register, you might suspect he is on drugs. But Tad would never take drugs, what with all the fresh air in the world! Tad and all his co-workers, Tad, wear matching vests adorned with loops and hooks. You may briefly wonder if the Tads go out after work wearing their matching vests, or if they're just part of a cult whose members love to fish. Tad is always happy and positive. The only time I've ever seen Tad a little bit down was when I told him I thought all sleeping bags were alike. Don't be sad, Tad! I know better now. Every food available at REI has the word "fiber" on the package, and everything else they sell has a tough or scary name: the Enforcers, the Prowlers, the Trail-blazers, the Strykers. No, these aren't names of military attack plans—they're just waterproof socks!

I was always one of those East Coast kids who refused to button my jacket. I was cold through most of the 1980s. In college, I wore a thin, vintage men's overcoat I got for twelve dollars at Screaming Mimi's—who thought about warmth? But now I was dating someone who grew up in the Midwest, where cold is no joke and where being prepared to face the elements is just something a person who isn't an idiot does. Peter knows everything there is to know about outdoorsy things like what to do if you see a bear (run? Don't run? I always forget), and if you want to talk about wind-resistance ratings or sweat-wicking properties, have I got the guy for you! He's also tried about a million times to explain to me why warm water makes ice cubes faster than cold water, which confounds me to such a degree that I respond by running around the house yelling, "I was an English major! I wrote my thesis on Tennyson!" But at REI, with the help of Peter and the Tads, I stocked up on thermals and a good ski jacket, plus socks called the Annihilators, the Doomsdays, and the Widow-Makers.

On our ski trip, I was warm and dry. And I realized for the first time in my life that feeling like your toes are going to fall off doesn't have to be part of being outside in the snow. I couldn't believe such comfort existed! I started buying so much outdoor athletic gear that I actually applied for an REI membership card. My bungee cords now earn points!

Whether it's on your own or through someone else, it's wonderful to be introduced to something you didn't realize you needed. In learning about the wonders of REI, it occurred to me that going into vulnerable public situations unprepared was a little like facing winter in New York City or being on the ski slopes with my twelve-dollar Screaming Mimi's coat flapping open. I wish I'd learned sooner, but in more ways than one, I now know more about protective layers than I used to. I've learned that a little readiness goes a long way when facing the elements, be they rain, or snow, or *Access Hollywood*. Just like in the outdoors, I've learned it's much easier to strip off a layer if you find you don't need it than to put one on. If you've already exposed yourself, it may be too late.

Peter has family in Northern California, and the first time I traveled with him there, I stopped short in the middle of the Sonoma County airport. There, in the center of the lobby, is a life-size Lucy advice booth with a sign that says THE DOCTOR IS IN. Charles Schulz was a native of the area, and *Peanuts* characters abound. The Lucy booth carries mostly travel pamphlets and maps to wine country, rather than advice for actors, but I still found its existence comforting, its appearance a positive sign.

Last week I opened the car door and one of Peter's golf balls rolled out and onto the street, and I thought, there was a time when this would have been a very big deal. Today my car not only has random golf balls in it, but also khaki-colored sun hats that resemble those worn by beekeepers, an assortment of bandanas, those sunglasses that are only meant to be used as protective eyewear during a racquet sport, and dog-eared paperback books of poetry. Now I take these items for granted. Back then, a man's golf ball rolling out of my car would have prompted frenzied calls to my girlfriends: "He left a golf ball in the car. He just *left* it there. What does it mean? WHAT DOES IT MEAN? Should I text him about it? I SHOULD, right? He's probably looking ALL OVER FOR IT." I wish I'd enjoyed my single days more and spent my free time reading or becoming a better photographer or something, and not worried so much about the meaning of golf balls.

Because here's the thing: I was fine on my own, and so are you. But it can be hard when you feel ready for Happy Couplehood and you seem to have missed the train. As my friend Oliver Platt used to say to me about hopes and dreams I'd share with him: "It's coming, just not on your time frame." I find this a helpful reminder in any number of ways: not only when you're hoping to meet someone, but also when you're waiting for a better job or for some relief during a bleak time. When Peter and I held hands that night all those years ago, I had no idea we'd end up shopping at REI together one day. It might have been nice if he could have turned to me and said:

"Look, tonight isn't the time, but we're going to leave here and learn a bunch of things that are going to make this work approximately five years from now—see you then!" But life doesn't often spell things out for you or give you what you want exactly when you want it, otherwise it wouldn't be called life, it would be called vending machine.

It's hard to say exactly when it will happen, and it's true that whatever you're after may not drop down the moment you spend all your quarters, but someday soon a train is coming. In fact, it may already be on the way. You just don't know it yet.

Labor Days

. . . .

I've been fortunate to work for many wonderful writers in television and film. I've done several classic plays and musicals, performed a handful of works by Shakespeare, and—while in graduate school—studied the works of Chekhov and Ibsen in depth. Which is why I feel confident in my ability to assure you that, without a doubt, the most challenging line of dialogue that's ever been conceived by an author to be performed by an actor is "Welcome to Chili's!" Hamlet, schmamlet—go ahead right now and try *that* line at home.

In that short phrase, you must convey happiness, wholesomeness, hospitality, cleanliness, family values, and a potato that's been well baked—all without a trace of cynicism. Undersell it and you risk coming off like a surly teen who was forced to take a job for the summer. Overdo it and you may seem haughty in a way that unintentionally conveys that you think this place is beneath you and that you're still angry about being passed over for the hostess position at the Olive Garden.

For years before I was ever cast in a "real" part, I auditioned for, and ended up making, many commercials. Some actors I knew at the time thought commercials were a bad pursuit. They felt they weren't artistic enough. Some worried the repetition of days spent holding up a jar of peanut butter and grinning crazily at it would give them bad habits as an actor. For me, I found that the routine of auditioning almost every day made me more able to handle my nerves when something bigger came up. I'd schlep into the city from Brooklyn with my giant book bag in which I always carried both a blue denim shirt (to play moms and other people who cared about detergent) and a black blazer (to play young professionals who tended to care more about cars and banks), and even if I didn't get the job, I felt I'd done something that day. I liked the feeling that I was working, even if it wasn't exactly *Hedda Gabler*. The only line I drew artistically was regarding feminine protection ads. I wasn't sure if I'd ever have any success as an actor, but even if not, I knew I didn't want to be immortalized on film riding a horse on a beach as the sun set feeling "fresh."

During this time, when I wasn't playing someone whose biggest worry in life was her dishpan hands, I frequently worked as a background player. This involved being paid approximately a hundred dollars to pretend to read the label on a tuna fish can in a fake grocery store aisle in the very distant background of a shot of the person who actually had been hired to bemoan *her* dishpan hands. In every single commercial I ever auditioned for, we were advised by the casting people to speak into the camera "like you're talking to your best friend." In life, if I ever spent longer than ten seconds talking about my dry hands, or how delicious a certain line of frozen entrées was (even with one-third fewer calories!), or how truly bouncin' and behavin' my hair was lately, I'd have no friends.

At the time, it was a struggle to stay afloat in Manhattan. (How times have not changed!) Occasionally I'd have a commercial run on air long enough to pay the bills for a few months, but I made a rule that I'd keep some sort of day job up until the time when acting became enough of a conflict that I had to quit. But as I licked fake toothpaste off my teeth for the millionth time, I wondered if that day would ever come.

Over a Labor Day weekend a few years ago, Peter and I were invited to a party at the home of Larry Owen, a professor of his in college. In honor of the holiday, Larry had asked everyone to write down all the jobs they'd ever done to make money. At the party, everyone shared their lists, and it made for some lively conversation. Some of Peter's jobs included snow removal, movie theater usher, and morning janitor at a place called the Chopstick Inn. He worked the fish-and-chips booth at the state fair, sold Time-Life books over the phone, and worked the night shift as a proofreader for Merrill Lynch. He delivered pizzas, worked as the pantry chef at a Bennigan's, and tended lawns for a landscaper. His least favorite job was insulating houses—he always went home feeling suspiciously itchy. One of his favorites was bartending on Broadway, where he got to see free theater and work alongside an unknown aspiring writer named Aaron Sorkin. (I wonder whatever happened to that guy.)

One summer in Peter's home state, Minnesota, he worked as a puppeteer with a mobile puppet stage. He'd hitch the puppet wagon to his car and drive from park to park, entertaining kids. One day the hitch came loose and the wagon tipped over, scattering puppets all across County Road C. The police arrived to survey the scene. "The paperwork on this is going to take a while," one of them said. Peter, nervous he was going to be late to his next gig, asked why. The cop nodded at the scattered puppet bodies. "We've got a lot of casualties here," he deadpanned.

In high school, I mucked out stalls at a barn in my neighborhood and drove a summer-camp school bus. (Yep, I replaced "drives a stick shift" with "licensed bus driver" on my résumé under special skills. Still—strangely—no takers.) One of my first steady jobs, the summer before my freshman year of college, was as a receptionist in a hair salon. That summer it was like I caught some sort of bug from watching people get their hair done all day. When I started that job my hair was down to the middle of my back, and by the time I was ready to head off to school I'd practically cut it all off. I've long since destroyed all the photos of me with that haircut—sadly for you—but to give you a sense of the situation, here's the picture I gave the stylist as inspiration for what I wanted:

Decades from now, historians will still be debating whether it was the freshman fifteen or the razor-sharp sideburns that kept me completely date-free that year!

During college I waitressed, ushered at an Off-Broadway theater, and spent Saturday nights on a folding chair in a closet as a coat check girl. I was an aide at a kindergarten, where I was obviously in way over my head, since—as you may remember—I skipped kindergarten and still had no idea what they did there. And I stacked books in the law library at Columbia, a job I chose specifically to meet guys but which turned out to be a total bust since, unlike the undergraduate libraries I'd been in, people actually studied there.

After college, I worked at Barney's New York, where I'd like to retroactively apologize for whatever you bought from me that I told you was the perfect thing to wear to your corporate law office. To this day I haven't been in too many of those, and back then I probably thought the neon pink hoodie and tassel-covered wedges would show not only that you were a good lawyer but, most important, that you were still "fun." I was also a cocktail waitress at a comedy club called the Improv on 46th Street. The excellent comic Dave Attell worked the door back then, and from the back of the dark room, in between slinging drinks, I watched a young Ray Romano perform stand-up. Now, whenever this comes up in conversation, Ray always asks me the same thing, forgetting that he's asked me already: "Did I hit on you?" Why, no, Ray, you did not. Even though my sideburns had totally grown in by then.

One summer during grad school I lived in Chicago. My friend Maria and I got jobs at the famous diner Ann Sather, where we worked behind the cinnamon roll counter every morning starting at five o'clock. We sold only two items— cinnamon rolls and coffee—so the days were usually pretty uneventful. But one day we looked up after the morning rush and noticed that someone had left behind an open purse on the counter with what looked like a big bag of cocaine in it. We peeked inside, searching for anything that might help us find the owner. It may seem weird that we went digging around in someone else's bag after we found drugs in it, but at first we weren't positive that's what it was, since neither of us had ever seen cocaine except in movies. But we finally came to the conclusion that yep, that's what it was, all right— how thrilling! We'd cracked this case wide open—this must be how Cagney and Lacey felt all the time! Just then a very pale and sweaty woman came up to the counter. "Um, excuse me. Did you find a, um ...?" she stuttered, eyes shifting around nervously. We nodded and handed her the bag. She stuffed a fifty-dollar bill in the tip jar and made a hasty exit. It didn't occur to us until later that giving someone their drugs back rather than calling the police is the literal definition of "aiding and abetting." Also, we decided that people who can afford giant bags of cocaine should really be embarrassed at leaving anything less than a cool hundy in the tip jar.

From the showcase my acting school class performed in New York after graduation, I finally scored an agent. But for a long time nothing came of the few auditions I got. So I taught SAT test prep, driving my rusty green Honda Accord out to places like Far Rockaway and Staten Island. I also worked for a catering company, demonstrated the Uno card game at the annual Toy Fair, and for one very long and clammy day wore a giant dog costume to play the mascot at a World Cup soccer convention. It took me half a day in the costume to realize there was no need for me to smile while taking photos with the attendees—they couldn't see my face through the giant head I was wearing, and anyway my grin was already painted across my face in furry black whiskers. Also—in case you were wondering—no, it does not feel good when someone gleefully knocks on the side of your doggie head and asks "if it's hot in there." Yes, sir. Yes, it is. Also, while I understand that your friends find it funny, please stop scratching me behind the ears.

Finally, after about three years of booking only commercials and a few lines on soap operas here and there, I was cast in a supporting part in a play at the George Street Playhouse in New Jersey—my first union job since my role as Blinky

McDryEyes in summer stock! I promptly turned in my apron at the Mexican restaurant I'd been working at in Park Slope, Brooklyn. My boss, Joe, was very nice about it; he told me I was welcome back anytime, which not only was cool of him but also proved he didn't know how many free margaritas I'd been giving away to all my friends. *Would* I be back? I wondered. Or was the day job portion of my career finally over?

I'd love to say that all those hours spent doing things I *had* to do in order to survive—in order to inch closer to the thing I very much *wanted* to do—also gave me usable skills that I carried forward with me in life. I'd like to tell you that thanks to that first real job and its resulting hideous haircut, Steven Spielberg stopped me on the street, demanding to know where I got my pointy sideburns and incredible acting ability. But that did not happen. The takeaway from my many jobs, as far as I can tell, is this:

1. Don't throw away hideous pictures of yourself—you may need to use them in your book one day.
2. Demand more money when returning drugs to strangers.
3. Dog costumes are very hot.
4. Oh, and thanks to that one summer I spent working at Benetton, I am, to this day, the guy to ask if you need your sweater neatly folded. Dozens of jobs, one actual skill!

At the Labor Day party, we all bonded over our shared tales of "that really awful job I had." Not all the stories were about terrible things that happened at work, but the best ones were. Maybe that's why you seldom see actors on talk shows regaling the hosts with stories of "that time I was well compensated at an early job I very much enjoyed." There's more comedy in failure than in success, and it's a much more universal language. At the party, the worst jobs also seemed to be the ones everyone felt most proud to have endured. It's an accomplishment to do something well, but maybe even a bigger one to do something well when you'd really rather not be doing it at all.

A few years ago I was back in my old neighborhood in Brooklyn, and when I turned a corner, there was my former boss, Joe, standing out in front of the Mexican restaurant as if no time had passed at all.

"Hey! I used to work here!" I said.

"I know," he said, like he'd just seen me bussing tables there yesterday.

"This was my last real job before I started working as an actor," I told him.

"I know," he said.

"I gave away a lot of free margaritas," I blurted out.

He rolled his eyes. "I know," he said again, but he was smiling. I looked inside the restaurant and saw that almost nothing had changed, which was oddly comforting. It made it even easier to picture myself there as I was in 1995, when I was scrappily patched together by green Dep gel, scrunchies, and stirrup pants. I realized that even though that restaurant hadn't been my dream job, I'd really liked working there. The rule I'd made for myself about keeping a day job until I could make a living acting was a good one. Wearing a dog costume was no fun, but I did it because it was more money than I usually made in a day, and I wasn't too proud to hustle.

Maybe that's why Professor Owen asked us to make those lists in the first place: to remember where we all started, and share stories of how far we'd come. To journey back to whatever each of our individual Brooklyns had been, and look in the window of the Mexican restaurant and remember ourselves as we were, young and hungry.

So, welcome to Chili's, y'all. Whether you're saying it for real or just trying to get the part, say it loud and say it proud.

Judge Not, Lest Ye Be a Judge on *Project Runway*

. . . .

My Life in Fashion

As you probably know, I am regularly featured on best-dressed lists, constantly praised for "owning it" and "killing it" on the red carpet, and have Zac Posen on speed dial. Wait. That's not me, that's Cate Blanchett! But obviously, in general, I'm a popular fixture on the fashion scene and can usually be spotted sporting free outfits sent to me by designers while sitting next to Anna Wintour in the front row of all the hottest runway shows during New York Fashion Week, before partying the night away with one to seven members of the Kardashian family. Wait. That's not me, that's Gigi Hadid! Wait. That's not her either, because she's a successful top model who is most likely to be walking *in* the show. Well, whoever's next to Anna in the front row is probably pretty psyched to be sitting in this place of honor. They're also probably hungry and their shoes are too tight. And whoever they are, they aren't me. But for some reason, I always forget that I'm not really a fashion-type person, and every once in a while I attempt to be one anyway. Who am I? When it comes to fashion, I'm not entirely sure.

My dad is six foot three, thin, and athletic, so even without him trying very hard, clothes look great on him. He was voted best-dressed in high school, even though he went to a Catholic school where they all wore uniforms, so I'm not exactly sure how it was that he distinguished himself, or why the school even bothered to assign that superlative to one of hundreds of boys wearing identical navy blue blazers. But what that says to me is that my father was so innately fashionable he somehow managed to look better-dressed than his classmates, even though they were all wearing the exact same thing.

So I suppose my dad was my first fashion idol, which is troubling only in that when I was a preteen girl I learned everything I first knew about what to wear from a tall preppy lawyer in his thirties. This was the 1980s in Washington, D.C., which meant my key pieces included wide-wale corduroys, L. L. Bean boat shoes, and anywhere from one to forty-seven shirts layered on top of one another with collars of varied jauntiness. My turtleneck was up and scrunchy, or sometimes neatly folded down! My Izod collar was down sometimes, unless of course it was up! This made for lots of fun choices, which in any combination ensured you were both overheated and bulky—you really couldn't go wrong.

After a while, rather than simply being influenced by my father's law office fashions and continuing to reinterpret them as a teen girl, I began to just cut out the middleman and wear his clothes. Back then, I really didn't like dresses. I remember having to buy a skirt for the eighth-grade band recital because I didn't own a single one. Fine, I was a tomboy. But here I am in one of my dad's starched white dress shirts, which he wore underneath his suits for work. So presumably all the extra length and bulk of a man's dress shirt is tucked into my (probably boys') Levi's corduroys, thereby obscuring any girl shape struggling to emerge from beneath.

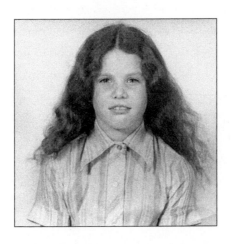

In the late 1970s and early 1980s, the Gap, where I got most of my dad-like clothes, was not yet the fashion-forward ubiquitous mall shop it has become, but more of a place where construction workers got their basics. Back then, they didn't even carry any of their own name-brand stuff. The Gap specialized in plaid flannel shirts by nameless designers and crunchy Levi's that had to be washed twenty to thirty times before they would stop standing up on their own. Luke Danes–type fashions. Skinny jeans didn't yet exist, but we knew enough to see that straight-leg jeans weren't as flattering as they could be, so some girls I went to school with had their jeans taken in along the inseam. I was too free-spirited (disorganized) for such tailoring frippery, so instead of sewing mine to make the leg narrower, I folded the jeans inward along the inseam, and I STAPLED THE TWO PARTS TO-GETHER. My look was stocky teenage boy meets Office Depot.

But I always liked the *idea* of fashion and of being fashionable, and as I got older I felt it was my responsibility to at least try—perhaps in part because of the trend toward actors being not just actors but also brands of some sort. It's not enough today just to be a good actor, it seems. One must also be a fashion icon, colon cleanse spokesperson, and designer of a line of plus-size dog costumes on the side. Your St. Bernard has been overlooked for too long!

In my family, there are several well-dressed ladies. My mother could take something odd from any sale rack and turn it into part of an elegant ensemble. My stepmother, Karen, and sister Maggie both have a great eye for patterns and fun accessories. My sister Shade always looks chic in her New York City color palette, which ranges from black to black. And my brother, Chris, like my dad, has a classic East Coast style. It's in my blood, or so I've tried to convince myself again and again. Those first twenty or so years of dad shirts and Stan Smith sneakers were my dormant phase, but I knew that Trendsetter Lauren was in there somewhere, just waiting to come out.

So when the call came one early summer day to be a judge on one of my favorite shows, *Project Runway*, I thought my fashion destiny had finally found me. Peter and I were spending the weekend in East Hampton, so not only was the call exciting in itself, but the whole request took on a beachy, Nancy Meyers–movie golden glow. Oh, oh, look at me! I walk barefoot on the beach, wearing a straw hat I paid nine million dollars for at Calypso on Main Street! I got this iced coffee at Once Upon a Bagel in Sagaponack! I vacation in the Hamptons! I'm a judge on *Project Runway*! Whose life is this— Bethenny Frankel's? After all those years of schlepping around Manhattan in my black puffy Reebok high-tops, I'm now positively killing it as a New Yorker!

The episode I'd been asked to do was the season ten premiere. I learned that Pat Field, the incredible stylist from *Sex and the City,* would also be a guest judge, along with the regular judges Michael Kors and Nina Garcia, and of course host and supermodel Heidi Klum. Just picturing the company I'd be keeping already made me feel better-dressed. I got to borrow a Michael Kors dress for the shoot, and I had fancy people doing my hair and makeup. This was unusual for me then, but I dreamed that in my new more fashionable life I'd be calling a day like that "Tuesday."

Because it was to be the first episode of the season, and an anniversary to boot, they set up a special runway in the middle of Times Square so that fans could be in the audience for a portion of the show. I was driven over to the location in a limo with Heidi, who was extremely friendly and welcoming. She waved from the open window and smiled for photos in the middle of Times Square. People were giddy to see her. Backstage, I met Tim Gunn, who was kind and gracious. "What a lovely way to start our season," he said upon meeting me. I blushed from head to toe.

The judges were then seated in a row of chairs near the

runway and handed index cards on which to write our comments. Heidi and Tim welcomed the audience and announced the start of the season. The crowd cheered. Loud music thumped through the outdoor speakers. The show began.

I guess what I remember most about the runway show was NOTHING I REMEMBER NOTHING OH GOD WHAT JUST HAPPENED. The show was over in what seemed like a blink. Prior to this night, my concept of a "show" involved popcorn or an intermission or perhaps complaints about the unnecessary length of that one scene in Act Two. This show was over before I even had time to become uncomfortable on my folding chair. Also (and this will come as a shock to absolutely no one) models make everything look great. I'd just watched a series of the most beautiful young women in the world walk by—who cared what they were wearing? Oh, supposedly me.

The other judges stood up and started musing about the show while, in a state of utter panic, I racked my brain for details, trying to come up with anything at all I could remember from the blur I'd just experienced. Um, okay, think, think. That one model was wearing . . . *pants,* I guess? Or were those actually pants? Or was it a *skirt* of some . . . no, pants, I think? These were my detailed fashion impressions. Then someone came to collect our index cards from us. I looked down at the cards in my hand and, heart pounding, realized I'd written almost nothing on them. "Wait, are we—these are their scores? We're turning in the scores *now*?" I said to Nina, dumbstruck.

"Yes," she said, totally friendly. "What did you think of the show?"

I grinned idiotically in a way I hoped looked haute couture, mumbled something like "Wow, it's—with the clothes, making!" and turned back to my blank cards. Hastily I wrote down as much as I could remember from what I'd just seen and assigned some scores randomly. Even now, I couldn't tell you what the scoring system is or even the range of numbers it involves. It's like I had a fashion-induced blackout. Was it 1–10? Or 0–100? The giant X's they use on *America's Got Talent*? I have literally no idea.

Once back in the studio, I calmed down a little. It was exciting to be on a set I found so familiar after having watched every episode. The judges have all worked together for years, so there was lots of laughter and chitchat as we waited to begin. Then, one by one, the contestants filed out to stand on the stage beside the models wearing their garments.

The first thing I noticed was how close we were to the contestants. Almost uncomfortably close. Much closer than it looks on television. Yet still too far away to make small talk. Whatever the distance is that makes those two things simultaneously possible is one I'd never experienced before. The effect of this strange faraway intimacy meant that everyone just sort of stared at each other without saying much in between critiques. Plus, in order to get those swoopy camera angles, they put the camera on a swoopy mechanical arm thing, and we were warned that the swooping takes a while. So between critiques, the camera flew around on its arm like some sort of drunk helicopter, getting reaction shots from each contestant, and then from the judges. They asked us to hold our reactions as best we could until they got to us. Ever smile for a photograph for someone who doesn't know how to work their camera? Twenty times longer than that. My mouth started to tremble from trying to hold a smile. During one of these awkward frozen moments, one of the contestants grinned at me and mouthed the words "I love you," and I tried as best I could to communicate my thanks while also maintaining my frozen mannequin face.

Unfortunately, when it came time for the judges to give their critiques, this same girl turned out to be in the bottom three. This part is also a bit of a blur, but from my many years as a viewer I'll guess Nina said something about a garment being reminiscent of "Dior in the seventies," Michael said a textile looked like a "frat house bath mat," and Heidi found one of the dresses "too sad." When it came to me, I tried my best to come up with an opinion that was also not an opinion. I think I said something like "Maybe the T-shirt is a little too ... *T-shirty*?" or something equally benign. But the girl who'd mouthed that she loved me looked as if I'd punched her, and that's when I realized the real problem I'd been having all evening was simply that I didn't like being a judge. I'd never judged anything in my life before. And even if I'd discovered I was an okay judge in general, even if I liked telling other people my opinions, the truth was that I wasn't really very qualified in this particular arena. If anyone at the show had seen how many pairs of sweatpants I had at home, they'd have shown me the door. My favorite outfits are jumpsuits. I buy too many. They always just seem like such a good idea at the time. I'm probably drawn to them because they remind me of my favorite childhood pajamas, but without the built-in slippers. There's one jumpsuit I wear that Peter calls my "that nice lady who works at the gas station" look. In fashion, I've always been more of a follower than a leader.

Here I'm copying not only my cousin Heather's wardrobe but also her bedhead chic hairstyle and rockin' smize. That's what a smize is, right?

I actually really love when I get to prepare for a big, over-the-top event that is seriously glamorous. I view the work of fashion designers like I do any art, and I get a kick out of occasionally dressing up in a big way. But being exposed to the world of a Big Night Out doesn't necessarily translate into real life. It's like learning how to make a soufflé, then being asked to put dinner on the table for five teenage boys on a Monday night: "I know you just got home from basketball practice, but would you guys mind waiting forty-five minutes to an hour for an airy and eggy dessert that isn't even filling?"

As a viewer of *Project Runway,* my favorite part has always been watching people create things, then following the decisions they made to see how they got to a finished product. In so many ways, that's the work of an actor too, and something I totally relate to. The judging was the least fun part. As a friend, I don't mind giving advice when I'm asked, but if you don't take it, I'm not going to ask you to clean up your work space and go home. I felt embarrassed too. I can't even stand giving feedback to the potato peeler I bought on Amazon— what made me think this would be any different?

For weeks after the show was over, I went on and on to all my friends about my runway show semi-blackout, how worried I still was about the nice girl and my "T-shirty" comment, and how in general my reaction to being a judge was much different from what I'd expected. I told them all about who got cut and why, what really went on behind the scenes, and what we had for dinner (everyone wants to know what models eat). One day I was telling my lawyer, Adam, my stories, and he stopped me midsentence. "Wait. It's just me you're telling all this to, right? I mean, you haven't been telling other people any of these stories, have you?" When I told him that yes, in fact, I had, because I was really, really traumatized by judging, he stopped me again. "Lauren," he said, with genuine concern in his voice, "you aren't allowed to talk about any of that. You signed a confidentiality agreement."

"Ugh, well, right," I tried to joke, "but I didn't actually *read* it that carefully—what do you think I have a lawyer for?"

He responded by telling me that everything I'd been saying was in total breach of my contract. Great. I was such a bad judge that now I might have to sit in front of a real one?

I pictured Tim Gunn, sad about having to testify against me: "Well, I *thought* it was a lovely way to start our season, but now . . ."

Over the years, I've gotten to do some pretty exciting things. Peter and I once made an appearance at the Macy's Thanksgiving Day Parade, where we got escorted through the crowds and massive balloons to have an up-close experience I'll never forget. I was flown to Amsterdam for a week to promote *Gilmore Girls*. I hosted the American Cinema Editors awards (the Eddies), where I got to fulfill my lifelong dream of delivering this piece of genius comedy: "Hey, who cut one?" I once rode the Disney jet when I was doing a series for ABC. I got to bring my friend Jen, and there was a marching band waiting for us on the tarmac when we arrived—not the usual way you expect to be greeted at work!

I've also been asked to do a lot of really unexpected things. One time I was invited to speak at a toilet paper convention. Another, to go on a morning show and discuss calcium supplements. Over the course of my career, I've gotten requests as odd and varied as promoting a line of cat food (I don't have a cat), being on the cover of a golf magazine (I don't play golf), and appearing on *Sesame Street* (I did this one! I know he's really famous, but guys, Grover is *so* down to earth in real life). I've learned that it's always nice to be invited to a party; there's just no way to know ahead of time what the party will be like.

In fashion, one day you're in, and the next day you're out. I was literally in for just the one day, but I realized I'm happier being out, or better yet, at home on my couch wearing sweatpants, watching as a fan.

Oh, and in case you were wondering, we ordered from a nice Japanese restaurant in Midtown, and Heidi had tofu in black bean sauce. Please remember how much you enjoyed that information, because I'm writing it to you from jail. This prison jumpsuit I'm wearing isn't as flattering as some of the ones I have at home, but that's okay.

I'll just have to make it work.

Someday, Someday, Maybe You'll Believe My Novel Wasn't Completely Autobiographical

. . . .

I was in Atlanta, and it was the night before we were about to start filming the movie *Middle School,* based on the books by James Patterson and Chris Tebbetts. At the cast dinner, I was thrillingly and frighteningly seated next to James Patterson himself—the author of countless thrillers, epic franchises that became Hollywood blockbusters, and a surprising number of children's books. So I couldn't help but ask him the question he's probably been asked a million times: "How do you do it?"

He turned to me and said, "Keep going, keep going, keep going."

Whoa. That pretty much says it all, I guess.

One day in 2011, I was sitting in my trailer after finishing a day of work on *Parenthood.* I had filmed a few scenes that morning, but we'd gotten through them fairly quickly. I'd already worked out that day, spoken to my dad, answered some emails, and had lunch. It was too early to start making dinner, and I didn't quite feel like going home yet. I realized that for the first time in what felt like years, I had something I almost never had: extra time on my hands. When I was in high school and college, there were always a million homework assignments due, projects I needed to work on, plays and musicals to rehearse. After school, out in the real world, there was also always something hanging over my head: making enough money to pay the rent, pounding the pavement all over New York, and, later, driving all over Los Angeles, trying to get people to hire me, trying to land somewhere even a little bit permanent so that I didn't wake up every morning with a pit in my stomach, wondering where my next paycheck was coming from. When I finally did land somewhere, on *Gilmore Girls,* there was hardly time to notice. The years I spent there were packed full: dialogue to memorize, long hours of filming, and all that went into publicizing the show. During the summers between seasons of the show, I hadn't wanted to rest either. I did movies and plays whenever I could, anxious to keep the momentum up. Keep going, keep going, keep going.

So that day in my *Parenthood* trailer, the realization that I had free time was an odd feeling, and an unfamiliar one. And there was something else too. For a moment I couldn't pin it down. It was almost as if someone else was in the room. Finally it came to me. It was a . . . voice, I guess? When it finally spoke, it asked me something unexpected.

Did you, um, make it? the voice whispered, surprised.

As a working actor, you're always being asked when it was that you finally knew you'd "made it." Most actors I know, myself included, respond with something resembling "never." Acting is such a precarious profession that most of us wisely never relax, never stop watching our backs, never feel we have true job security. Even if the evidence is to the contrary, most of us feel we aren't yet safe. If necessary, I could pick up a tray tomorrow and take your order—I remember those years like no time has passed. I never take this career for granted. There are far more actors who worked for a while and disappeared than there are actors who've stuck around for decades.

So when I tell you that a whispery voice in my ear asked me if I'd "made it," I don't at all mean in the red-carpet interviewer sense. I don't mean it as in I saw my face on the side of a bus, or I won an award, or I just bought my fourth Ferrari. And it was then I knew I'd made it! I mean it in a subtler sense. The voice suggested that maybe the time had come to accept that I didn't have to wake up every day with ulcer-inducing terror over where my next meal was coming from. Again, this was in 2011. I'd been supporting myself steadily as an actor since 1996, and the idea that maybe this was going to work out after all was occurring to me for the very first time. Actors: how therapists stay in business!

I mean, what was I thinking back then, when I decided to go into acting? Really, who did I think I was? *Show business?* Who does that? Starting out, I hadn't known anyone with even the vaguest connection to this mysterious world.

In high school, I had the lead in the musical my junior year (You remember *Hello, Dolly!*) but didn't get the lead my senior year, and I remember thinking, I've peaked. It's all over. So I wondered what had kept me going after that, through thousands of rejections and with no way of knowing I'd be sitting in a trailer on the Universal lot one day twenty years later with my bills relatively paid and time on my hands.

I pictured the brownstone in Brooklyn I'd lived in after grad school with Kathy, my best friend from college. I remembered some of the jobs I'd taken to make ends meet: catering and waitressing and working as a tutor, answering phones as a temp and trying to sell CPR lessons over the phone. I kept all my appointments in a Filofax day planner, pagers were considered novel technology, and Times Square was still full of X-rated movies. Things had changed so much since then. *I* had changed so much. Far from being asked about "making it," I'd found that the question that came up most often back then was some version of "When will you be giving this ridiculous pipe dream up?" Back then, I'd asked myself this with alarming frequency as well. When you have no credits on your résumé, there's no proof yet one way or the other. There's no way to know if the time you're spending will someday prove to be time you spent paying your dues or time you spent fooling yourself.

While I didn't want to write about myself exactly, I wondered if maybe a story of dreaming big, growing up, and forging a career was sort of universal. I hadn't given myself a time limit as an actor, but others I know did, and it occurred to me that might create a ticking clock that would help structure the story. I opened a Word document and started a ... what? I didn't even know what it was yet.

It turned out to be a novel. *Someday, Someday, Maybe* is about a young girl named Franny Banks who comes to New York City to follow her dream of becoming an actress. Aided by the pages of her Filofax date book, we follow a year in her life (sort of like *A Year in the Life*!), at the end of which she's vowed to give up and move back home if she doesn't find success. Set in the 1990s, it takes place in a New York City that has changed a great deal since then. The first thing I wrote was an anxiety dream that Franny has the night before an audition. It ended up also being one of the first things I cut. But over the next few weeks, I just kept going, kept going, kept going. It was a thrilling novelty to have something I could work on just by myself. I didn't need a set or a script or another actor. I loved my main character, Franny, of course, but it was just as fun to create the others. My friend Kathy was sort of the inspiration for Jane, but then Jane started taking on a life of her own. James Franklin, a bad-boy type whom Franny falls for, wasn't based on anyone in particular. He was inspired by some of the very actor-y actors I've known and have always been intrigued by, the ones who seem like they're never not playing the character of "extremely deep artiste." Barney Sparks, Franny's first agent, was nothing like any agent I ever had. I just liked the idea of her starting out with someone who'd been in the business a long time and who spoke in clichés that were also sincerely heartfelt. So while my original inspiration was personal, it wasn't really "about" me. Even if I'd wanted to use more details from my life at the time, I didn't keep a diary and my memory isn't that good. And when I started working on it, I had no particular goal in mind. It wasn't a calculated play to cash in on some backstory of mine. I was just enjoying trying something new that was creative, something that allowed me to connect with another time and place.

In fact, I went out of my way to make the characters *not* resemble anyone from my real life. I would never want the real people I work with to feel parodied or exploited. It's one of the things that slowed me down considerably on my second novel (more on that in a moment). I'd think, oh, a fun character would be an outspoken publicist who's always sending Franny to D-list events in order to "get seen." But then I don't want anyone to assume I'm parodying the publicist I'm working with, who's a man, so maybe I'll change the publicist to a woman. But, I don't want anyone to think I'm making fun of that one female publicist . . . You see the problem.

The first hundred pages just spilled out. They were a pleasure and a breeze, and to date that's the last time writing anything has ever come so easily. One day I mentioned to my agent that I'd been working on something, just for fun, and he asked me to send it to him, which I did, with apologies. It was very rough, I told him. I hadn't even proofread it for typos, I told him. But he read my scrappy pages and, without telling me, forwarded them to one of the best and best-known book agents at ICM and in the galaxy, Esther Newberg.

I'd only met Esther once, years before. Since then I've come to know her as an excellent dinner date and raconteur. Esther is smart, stylish, and a devoted Red Sox fan. But what I knew about her then was mostly that she hailed from the No Bullshit School of Agenting. (This should be an actual school—someone call *Shark Tank*!) Many agents have attended its sister campus, the Amazing Amazing School, a related but very different institution where even the three lines you had on that Friday night sitcom were so impressive they should earn you an Emmy. These agents are pleasant to deal with, but their comments require some translation on your part. Over time, you learn that "you're amazing" means you're just okay, "the ratings are great" means your show is getting cancelled, and "you look fantastic" means you've gained weight. I'll write it all up for you in another helpful chart! No Bullshit is by far my favorite school.

My conversation with Esther went something like this:

ESTHER: I read your pages.

ME: Oh, wow, really? They're not even—

ESTHER: I can get you a lot of money if I sell this book to certain people.

ME: Are you kidding? That's great! I mean, I wasn't even doing it for the—

ESTHER: But I don't want to sell it to those people.

ME: Oh, no? Uh, okay.

ESTHER: Because you know what else these people would buy from you?

ME: No, I don't—

ESTHER: Monkey doodles.

ME: Monkey . . . ?

ESTHER: Yes. From you, they'd buy a book of monkey crayon doodles. They'd buy a cookbook covering just nuts. They'd buy the confessions of your split ends. And you know why?

ME: Um, no . . .

ESTHER: The *Today* show. [Hi, Tamryn!]

ME: The *Today* show? [Hi, Willie!]

ESTHER: The *Today* show. [Hi, Carson! Filling in again, Jenna?] You can get booked as a guest on the *Today* show. [Hi, Al!] You can get a spot on *Ellen*. Books are hard to sell, and you have these ways to promote a book, and that's the main reason these certain people would buy your book. I don't want to sell this book to those people.

ME *(deflated)*: Oh, okay. Makes sense, I guess. Well, thanks anyway, I really appre—

ESTHER *(mysteriously)*: But there are other people.

ME: Other . . . ?

ESTHER: Well, there are three. Three other people.

ME: In all of publishing?

ESTHER: Three people—editors, I mean—whom I would trust with this. Three people who would only take it on because they believed in you and the book. But if one of them doesn't take it, I think we should wait. Unless you want me to call the monkey doodle people . . .

ME: No, no. I wasn't even—I was just sitting in my trailer one day and—

ESTHER: Well, then, we'll see what the people say.

ME: Okay! Let me just clean up the pages first, and—

ESTHER: I already sent the pages to the people.

ME: You already—

ESTHER: I'll let you know. *(Click.)*

Suddenly my solo trailer project had become a new way in which I'd potentially set myself up for more rejection. Suddenly I was waiting to see if I'd be accepted into another competitive world where people I'd never met would have opinions about my work. Why didn't I pick up knitting?

Why didn't I take a sailing class instead? Pottery? Why was I torturing myself? I felt nervous and neurotic. Would I be accepted? Maybe we *should* call the monkey doodle people? After all, an entire cookbook of nut recipes wasn't a *terrible* idea. And maybe my split ends would be healed if only they had the chance to speak out!

Writers: how therapists buy summer homes.

I don't remember if all three editors were interested. (Two were. I think three? Let's say they all were. Who can stop me? It's my book—I'm drunk with power!) But the proposal letter sent by my current editor, Jennifer E. Smith, jumped out at me, and made her the clear choice.

Jen is a talented YA author. She's from Chicago. She talks very fast. When Jen and I first met in person, I told her the story of writing my senior thesis as an English major in college. I confessed that I turned it in late after writing it directly in a word processor and correcting my typos and mistakes with Wite-Out. I just barely scraped by, deadline-wise. Jen—who was also an English major—laughed but looked slightly spooked by this information. She admitted to me that she was so well organized in college that she finished her senior thesis two weeks early, but she lied about it and pretended to still be working up to the deadline because she didn't want her friends to feel bad or think she was too much of a geek.

She may have been concerned about my deadline issues, but I thought this made us the perfect match. Ever see a buddy movie where one guy is the ne'er-do-well loose cannon and the other guy is too? No? Exactly. What's the fun of the ne'er-do-well loose cannon without the buttoned-up friend/brother/other cop who's trying to ensure he stays within the law? I was the Eddie Murphy to her Nick Nolte! The Bruce Willis to her Sam Jackson! The Hooch to her Turner! Sorry—it seems I stopped going to the movies in 1989.

The good news was that I'd been paired with an ideal partner. The bad news was that the minute I sold the book and it became an assignment with a deadline and people counting on me, I sort of froze up. This resulted in writing sessions where I stared at the blank computer screen with my heart thumping and a metallic taste in my mouth—my new definition of the boots of time marching all over me. To cope, I went down Google rabbit holes involving outdoor patio furniture and artisanal Korean pepper sauces. I'd write three lines, erase four, and look up which fish sauce to use when making nuoc cham. (Red Boat 40°N, 50°N if you can find it. Nuoc cham is a Vietnamese dipping sauce that calls for sambal oelek, an Indonesian chili paste, but I also sometimes use the Korean chili paste gochujang, and I find if you chop the ginger very fine you can—NOW DO YOU SEE WHY MY BOOK TOOK SO LONG? Also, the best time to buy patio furniture on sale is at the end of the summer or early fall. Spring is when they get you!)

Jen has become a friend as well as an invaluable person in my work life. Sometimes she tells me I need to throw something out. Sometimes she tells me I need to dig deeper. But early on, the main challenge was simply getting me to fill up more pages. "Just give me something," she'd say. "Don't worry too much. If you hit a rough patch, skip over it. You can go back and make it perfect later, but first you need a draft. I can't edit a blank page." Eventually I learned that, in the beginning at least, it was better for me to be finished than to try to be perfect. I had to get out of my own way. It wasn't that the voice in my head—the one telling me my pages weren't good enough—went away, exactly. I just didn't let it stop me. An important tool against self-doubt is just to ignore it. Forge ahead anyway. Just keep going, keep going, keep going.

I gave myself the goal of writing one thousand words a day. Sometimes I hit it, sometimes not. I had no routine—I wrote at work between scenes, at the kitchen table, on airplanes. My process was nonlinear and often chaotic. If I hit a scene or a plot point that stumped me, I'd put the missing scene in bold so I would remember to come back to it later: **Dan wedding scene to come.** Sometimes I didn't even know what the missing scene might be: **Franny says blah blah something here.** Talk about medical, medical!

I was filling every free minute, working harder than I had in years. So it was surprising that when I told people I was writing a novel, the two questions I got most often were "Is anyone helping you?" and "Are you doing that all by yourself?" You know, the same questions male authors get asked! I guess there is a tradition of memoirs sometimes being ghost-written. (Chuck—make sure this part *really* seems like I wrote it. And remind me to delete this note!) But fiction? There seemed to be some bias I couldn't quite put my finger on.

The book was far from perfect, but eventually it was done. Letting go of it was the strangest thing. I'd feel happy with a passage one week, but a week later I'd find things about it I wanted to change. I realized that the practice of writing the book had actually, slowly and over time, made me a better writer. So I'd see parts that I'd done months back and realize I could now do better. Which meant I wanted to keep revising. But when does the revising end? I'd committed to a publishing date, for one thing, but even if I hadn't, at some point you have to let it go or it isn't a book for sale, it's a pile of papers on your desk. The actor equivalent of this would be to film a scene, then watch it and think, why'd I do that with my hands? That shirt isn't flattering, I'm not as connected as I could be—let's go back and do it again. You could keep improving that one scene over and over, but the movie would never get made. "I'm going to pull this out of your hands now," Jen finally said.

Promoting the book was a new experience too. I did some signings at bookstores and got to be interviewed onstage by Anna Quindlen, one of my favorite authors. I was asked to (forced to) join Twitter, which I dreaded at first, but have come to (mostly) enjoy. I figured doing interviews would be the least revelatory experience, since I was used to those. But in subtle ways, I found the same "Who helped you?" tone was back once again.

The biggest example of this was an interview I did with a national newspaper. For starters, the journalist came to the interview a bit gruff. He didn't seem particularly familiar with my work or generally psyched to be there. It was a lunch interview, and he seemed annoyed at having to order something. I decided that I'd win him over with my sparkling personality! This is a very bad way to start an interview. You are not there to entertain like a clown at a kid's birthday party. Actually, maybe that's not a bad analogy. This party was about to turn a little scary and maybe even end in tears.

The interview was conducted more like a scene from *Law & Order* in which I was the perp and he was trying to trap me into making a confession. He opened up his notebook and methodically went down his list of questions.

HIM: On page 9 of your book, Franny has trouble with her curly hair. I read that *you've* had trouble with *your* curly hair.

ME: Yes, well, a bad hair day is sort of something many women can relate—

HIM: On page 11, Franny waitresses. Have *you* ever waitressed?

ME: Yes. Many actors, when they're starting out—

HIM: On page 39, Franny has an audition that doesn't go well. Have *you* ever had an audition that didn't go well?

ME: Yes, well, it's a book about a girl who wants— FINE! I DID IT OKAY? JUST HANDCUFF ME NOW.

Fairly quickly I felt he'd written the article before I ever showed up. I don't mean this literally, but he might as well have. He'd decided that my fiction was nothing more than a bunch of thinly veiled diary entries, and therefore deemed it unworthy—not "real" writing. I could have just stayed home in my pajamas.

I didn't need him to pat me on the head and tell me I'd done a good job. I didn't even need him to like what I'd written. But this wasn't supposed to be an article reviewing the book. This was supposed to be an article about the process and how the book came to be, and I found it strange that he'd come prepared mostly to dismiss the accomplishment itself.

"Thanks for doing this," I singsonged in an overly cheery tone as he left.

"Don't thank me until you've read it," he grumbled over his shoulder.

What was it I'd encountered that day, and those other times? Why would anyone assume I'd need help with, or take credit for, something that wasn't my work? Was it . . . *sexism*? In my Hollywood life, the sexism is so rampant that it's easy to spot. Every single feature film I've ever done was directed by a man, for example. Women who are hotter than me get parts I am up for all the time. What am I going to do—sue the Screen Actors Guild because I'm not Megan Fox? It is what it is. I do what I can to effect change within the system. But this brand of condescension was something new, and seemed woman-specific somehow. Maybe it had to do with being an actress, a job some people think is full of pretty dumdums. Male actors don't seem to face the same bias. Even though my former boss Ron Howard practically grew up on sets, when he was first starting out as a director I doubt anyone ever asked who "helped him" direct Tom Hanks in *Splash*.

In contrast, a few months after the book was published, I got word that Ellen DeGeneres's production company, AVGP, wanted to option it for television. There were discussions about who should write the script. Some advised me to stay open to suggestions, that to give the book its best shot at being made into a TV show it should probably be adapted by someone who'd actually written a TV script before. This made complete sense to me. But when I sat down with Ellen and her producing partner, Jeff Kleeman, and asked whom they were thinking of to do the adaptation, they looked at me funny. "You," they said, like it was the most obvious answer. That one word opened so many doors.

Now, that script was a delight to work on, but it didn't get picked up at the CW, so both opinions about who should write it probably had merit. But that experience led to a chance to write a pilot the next year, and that led to a feature agent at my agency taking an interest in me, which led to the opportunity to adapt the book *The Royal We* with my producing partner and husband, Mae Whitman. When Mae and I went to pitch the book to Terry Press, the head of CBS films, Terry looked at me and said: "Who's going to write it— you?" I nodded, and she said "Okay," giving me another first chance to do something I'd never done before.

I guess what I'm saying is, let's keep lifting each other up. It's not lost on me that two of the biggest opportunities I've had to break into the next level were given to me by successful women in positions of power. If I'm ever in that position and you ask me, "Who?" I'll do my best to say, "You" too. But in order to get there, you may have to break down the walls of whatever it is that's holding you back first. Ignore the doubt—it's not your friend—and just keep going, keep going, keep going.

Oh, and in case you were wondering, writing *Someday, Someday, Maybe* in the first place led to the book you're reading right now. And all of those other writing assignments, plus the filming of *Gilmore Girls: A Year in the Life,* are why the next novel is taking so long. But don't worry. In the meantime, you can pre-order my next book, *Monkey Doodles,* coming soon to a store near you!

Kitchen Timer

. . . .

Later in this book I write about the many wonders of returning to *Gilmore Girls,* but here's an early example of the kind
of mysterious and magical thing that sometimes occurred
during the filming of the reboot.

This time last year, I was an unemployed actor who'd recently said goodbye to a TV show. There's always a confusing
transition when a show ends, especially one as enjoyable as
Parenthood. The end of any job, especially a long-running one,
puts you in a kind of fog. I wandered around having trouble
making simple decisions, like should I work out first today or
drop off the dry cleaning? Dry cleaning first, right? Yeah, that's
the way people normally—no, maybe work out first? You go
from having your days completely regimented to everything
suddenly being up to you, and it's jarring. I wondered about
things my brain hadn't had time to ponder while working—
like how people do that thing with their hands where they

connect their fingertips in a way that makes the heart shape. You know that thing—it's in ads and on book covers (hi, Sarah Dessen!) and in commercials, and everyone knows about it, right? Well, no one did that when I was growing up. I never saw it before, say, the last ten years. Maybe it just wasn't a thing where I lived. But I'm pretty sure no one I knew anywhere did it. Could it be possible we've been on the planet this long and yet we only just thought of it? And if so, what took us so long? Doesn't this deep thought just blow your mind? Now you have something to talk about at the dinner table tonight.

The problem is that this kind of ungrounded period isn't great if you have, say, a writing assignment or three you're supposed to be working on. I was inching toward the finish line on a few things when I really needed to be footing or mile-ing it in that direction. Instead, my mind meandered over topics such as "Do you ever wonder why people in Los Angeles cross the street so slowly but people in New York City always sort of jog-run?" But life can't stay a *Seinfeld* rerun forever. Eventually, whether you're ready or not, limbo comes to an end because you must meet the deadline, or you have to get back to work, or, at the very least, because the aimless wandering phase is replaced by another actor favorite, the "IT'S OVER IT'S ALL OVER I'LL NEVER WORK AGAIN" phase.

But as *Gilmore Girls: A Year in the Life* began, there was suddenly a pileup of due dates the likes of which I'd never experienced before. First, without much notice, I was back to filming—and not those cushy *Parenthood* hours either. I wasn't sleeping in a bison carcass like Leo or anything, but I had suddenly returned to a very heavy workload. Obviously, this book was due. Not to mention the book that was due before this book was due. Then Mae and I sold *The Royal We,* and now that script was due too. I wished I could get back all the days I'd spent looking at vintage tile tables on Chairish and weighing the pros and cons of what time of day to drop off dry cleaning. Back then I'd had too much time on my hands; now I had too little.

One morning in the makeup trailer I was talking to Dan Bucatinsky, who plays Jim Nelson, the real-life editor of *GQ* magazine, in the show. He's also a screenwriter, and his book *Does This Baby Make Me Look Straight?* is a hilarious and heartfelt memoir about adoption and being a gay dad. For a while we just dished and shared writer woes. I talked about the various projects I was juggling and my worry over making my deadlines. Then I said something out loud that I'd never quite articulated before: "I know I'll get them done; I just really wish I had a less painful process."

Dan dipped his chin down to peer at me over his glasses. "Lauren," he said in a tone that also meant *puh-lease,* "call Don."

Remember Don Roos and *M.Y.O.B.,* the show I was on when I first got *Gilmore Girls*? Don Roos, the co-creator of *Web Therapy,* the writer of the screenplays *Marley and Me* and *Happy Endings* and *Boys on the Side*? Well, Don and Dan happen to be married. Don is funny and smart and I admire his work, and he's been a successful screenwriter for a long time. He must be doing something right. So I called him, figuring at the very least we'd have a fun lunch, even if he couldn't help with my procrastination problems.

I could have easily spent months and years staring at blank documents and staying up all night as I trial-and-errored my way through a few finished pages and many more images of vintage tile tables. But in the magical way that things just kept falling into place over the course of returning to the show, my question was answered on the very first try.

I had lunch with Don, and he explained his way of working to me, a method that's been so effective he actually wrote it up to give to the many writers he mentors. It's his variation on the Pomodoro technique, called Kitchen Timer, and it's transformed the way I write—I now spend fewer hours being way more productive. It gave me structure where there was none. It has changed my life as a writer, and I hope it changes yours too. I love it so much that it makes me want to touch my fingertips together in that wonderful symbol we just invented in the last decade. (But seriously, what took us so long?)

KITCHEN TIMER

The principle of Kitchen Timer is that every writer deserves a definite and doable way of being and feeling successful every day.

To do this, we learn to judge ourselves on behavior rather than content. We set up a goal for ourselves as writers that is easy, measurable, free of anxiety, and, above all, fail-proof, because everyone can sit, and an hour will always pass.

HERE'S HOW IT WORKS:

1. Buy a kitchen timer, one that goes to 60 minutes. Or use a timer app. Or tell Siri to start a timer for 60 minutes.
2. We decide on Monday how many hours of writing we will do Tuesday. When in doubt or under pressure or self-attack, we choose fewer hours rather than more. A good, strong beginning is one hour a day, but a half hour is also good, or twenty minutes. Some of us make appointments in our calendar for these hours, as if they are lunch meetings or business calls.
3. The Kitchen Timer hour:

    No phones. No texts. We silence ringers; we turn our phones facedown. It is our life; we are entitled to one hour without interruption, particularly from loved ones. We ask for their support. "I was on an hour" is something they learn to understand. But they won't respect it unless we do first.

    No music with words, unless it's a language we don't understand. Headphones with a white noise app can be helpful.

    No Internet, absolutely. We turn off our computer's Wi-Fi.

    No reading.

    No pencil sharpening, desk tidying, organizing.

4. Immediately upon beginning the hour, we open two documents: our journal, and the project we are working on. If we don't have a project we're actively working on, we just open our journal.

5. An hour consists of TIME SPENT KEEPING OUR WRITING APPOINTMENT. That's it. We don't have to write at all, if we are happy to stare at the screen or the page. Nor do we have to write a single word on our current project; we may spend the entire hour writing in our journal. Anything we write in our journal is fine; ideas for future projects, complaints about loved ones, what we ate for dinner, even "I hate writing" typed four hundred times.

When we wish or if we wish, we pop over to the current project document and write for as long as we like. When we get tired or want a break, we pop back to the journal.

The point is, when disgust or fatigue with the current project arises, we don't take a break by getting up from our desk. We take a break by returning to the comforting arms of our journal, until that in turn bores us. Then we are ready to write on our project again, and so on. We use our boredom in this way.

IT IS ALWAYS OKAY TO WRITE EXCLUSIVELY IN OUR JOURNAL. In practice it may rarely happen that we spend the full hour in our journal, but it's fine, good, and right if it does. It is just as good a writing day as one spent entirely in our current project.

6. It is infinitely better to write fewer hours every day than many hours one day and none the next. If we have a crowded weekend, we choose a half or quarter hour as our time, put in that time, and go on with our day. We are always trying to minimize our resistance, and beginning an hour on Monday after two days off is a challenge.

7. When the hour is up, we stop, even if we're in the middle of a sentence. If we have scheduled another hour, we give ourselves a break before beginning again--to read, eat, go on errands. We are not trying to create a cocoon we must stay in between hours (the old "I'm sorry, I can't see anyone or leave my house--I'm on a deadline" method). Rather, *inside* the hour is the inviolate time.

8. If we fail to make our hours for the day, we have scheduled too many. Four hours a day is an enormous amount of time spent in this manner, for example. If on Wednesday we planned to write two hours and didn't make it, we schedule a shorter appointment for the next day. We don't add an hour to "make up" or "catch up." We let the past go and move on.

9. When we have fulfilled our commitment, we make sure we credit ourselves for doing so. We have satisfied our obligation to ourselves, and the rest of the day is ours to do with as we wish.

10. A word about content: This may seem to be all about form, but the knowledge that we have satisfied our commitment to ourselves, the freedom from anxiety and resistance, the stilling of that hectoring voice inside us that used to yell at us that we weren't writing enough--all this opens us up creatively.

Good luck!

Don Roos

Parenthood Is the Best Neighborhood

. . . .

Don't you hate it when one of your friends starts dating someone fabulous, or gets a cool new job or an unexpected promotion, and they're so excited and happy and they can't stop talking about how lucky they are and how amazing everything in their life is, and generally just won't shut up about it? That's what me telling you about the experience of doing the show *Parenthood* is going to be like.

Lauren, please. You could never be as annoying as that.

But allow me to try.

We already know that I have a very special relationship that blossomed at work, which may seem like good fortune enough, but it doesn't stop there. I also fell in love with every other cast member there. As TV siblings, we didn't really resemble one another, but I so enjoyed the days we spent together, and the dance parties on the set with Peter and Dax Shepard and Erika Christenson. My pretend in-laws Monica Potter and Joy Bryant and Sam Jeager were, as people and actors, a fun and impressive bunch. The kids of *Parenthood* were gracious and sweet and smart, each and every one. Craig T. Nelson and Bonnie Bedelia were perfect as our fearless leaders—I grew up admiring their movies, so getting to work with them was even better. And I have a very special bond with my TV children, Mae Whitman and Miles Heizer; when we go out to eat, we still call it "family dinner."

I loved the writers and directors and my boss, Jason Katims, who was the person responsible for establishing this wonderful environment in the first place. Our assistant directors (ADs) kept the schedule running smoothly, and were kind and funny and pretended not to notice if I was late for my call time. Larry Trilling, one of our executive producers, is a guy I knew from college, and he became an even better friend at work. The whole place truly had a family feel.

Our cameramen were also vital to the success of the show. They helped illuminate our work by focusing on behavior they found interesting: someone's hands drumming nervously on a table, a subtle eye roll between spouses, Zeek puffing gleefully on his cigar. In most cases our scenes were shot proscenium style, meaning the action took place on one plane, with two or three cameras filming across from us, almost as if we were on stage. This gave the actors an incredible amount of freedom—much more than a regular television setup allows—and it made room for a great deal of collaboration.

Well, the people may have been great, but we've all watched enough Access Hollywood *to know that the work hours that go into making a sixty-minute show are grueling, right?*

Sorry. Can't help you there. The hours on *Parenthood*

were some of the best I've ever had. Within the excellent framework of the scripts we were given, we were also allowed some freedom with regard to dialogue. This meant we never got bogged down in having to do take after take, needing to say every single word exactly as written. This was especially helpful during our large family dinner scenes, and added to the texture of what a big family sounds like—people talking over each other in a messy, authentic way. We were aided in this by the work of our excellent sound department. I had to go in and rerecord a line maybe three times in six years, which is remarkably rare. In fact, everything ran so well, and we finished early on so many days, that in our last two seasons they actually cut a *whole day* out of our production on each episode, yet we still managed to finish at a reasonable hour. I wrote an entire book in my trailer during my free time. Monica Potter launched a beautiful line of home goods. Dax Shepard wrote and directed a film. Joy Bryant started a clothing line. Erika Christensen cycled seventy million miles across the city. We had satisfying jobs that also gave us room to grow, travel, and have lives.

To an exceptional degree, there was thought and care put into our well-being. The catering was excellent. Some days we had a vegan chef, on other days a Hawaiian poke bar. There was a smoothie station and freshly baked cookies every day at lunch. Once in a while we'd have an In-and-Out truck (awesome burgers), Kogi truck (Roy Choi's tasty Korean fusion tacos), or Van Leeuwen artisanal ice cream cart as a special treat. There was a costume parade on Halloween, carol singers at Christmas, and on our last day of the year a mariachi band during lunch to send us off.

Harrumph. This is somewhat irritating. They do not do these things at my job.

But wait, there's more! As part of the season five finale, a few of us got to go to *Hawaii* and stay at the Four Seasons hotel in Maui! Peter and Monica filmed for a few hours while I sipped mai tais by the pool!

Okay, you're right, this is starting to be a little sickening.

I'm not finished! Add to that the incredible stories we got to tell. Our show was about family and relationships, subjects that are about to become against the law on network television unless the family is also full of tattooed serial killer zombie firefighters who live in Chicago. Plus I got to work not only with my incredible TV family but also with fun guests like Billy Baldwin and Jason Ritter and Ray Romano. Which reminds me: I have a fear that I've already gone through all the tall actors in Hollywood and there may be none left to play my love interests in things. It's unusual to find very tall actors here—more of them than you might guess are really handsome shorties secretly standing on apple boxes. I'm five foot nine, so this is a serious matter of career survival for me, and I'm afraid I've already worked with more than my fair share of guys I can literally look up to: Dax and Peter and Craig and Sam from *Parenthood* are all unusually tall, Scott Patterson and David Sutcliffe and Scott Cohen on *Gilmore Girls* could have started a basketball team, and Joel McHale, whom I did *A Merry Friggin' Christmas* with, is a hilarious and muscly giant whose massive arms could double as legs. How long can this lucky streak really continue? I think Liam Neeson might be the only suitably sized actor left. Talk about turning tables, Mr. Neeson; this time it is *I* who will be coming after *you*!

Lauren, you've sort of gone off topic here. . . .

Ah yes, let me return to bragging. Like *Gilmore Girls, Parenthood* was another show that was a "people are happy to see you at the airport" show. It is an enjoyable perk of the job to see people's faces light up when they run into you, and maybe you get to hear a story of how something on your show reminded them of something good in their own lives. I wouldn't know, but I'm guessing this is preferable to them running away from you screaming, "Meth! Meth! So many years of meth!"

I think I've had enough. Can you please just think of one negative thing to say about working there?

Um . . . huh . . . let me see . . . Oh, I know! The Universal lot is off Lankershim Boulevard, which is one exit farther from my house on the 101 freeway than Warner Brothers, where we shot *Gilmore Girls.* So it took me about three minutes longer to get to work in the morning. Oh, the hardship I endured with these people!

PHOTO: © SHAWN BRACKBILL

Look Up!

. . . .

A Note from Your Friend Old Lady Jackson

Old Lady Jackson is a character I made up when I started catching myself giving advice—initially to Mae and Miles on the *Parenthood* set—that sounded like it came from your gray-haired grandma who spends her days in a rocking chair knitting you scratchy socks you pretend to love at Christmas. By creating this character, who was obviously very, very, very far away from myself, I hoped to confuse Mae and Miles, among others, into thinking that while I might sometimes seem to offer suggestions that could be considered a tad "old-timey," they weren't actually coming from me; they were really coming from this weird, remote other persona, and I was actually still very hip and relevant and wore my L. L. Bean duck boots ironically, and of course I knew who Tegan and Sara were (but only because Miles made me a CD).

When I started feeling older than my co-stars and other younger friends—some of whom were in their teens and early twenties—it was not in the normal ways I would've expected, like getting up from a chair and exclaiming "Oy, my hip!" For me, it started when my mention of *Happy Days* was met with a blank stare, and I couldn't convince anyone that the AOL pager had ever been a "thing." Because I live in Hollywood and am contractually bound never to age, instead of shouting "Your generation doesn't understand anything!" and stalking off to use the landline to call my answering service, I'd just roll my eyes and say, "I don't mean to sound like Old Lady Jackson here, but do you really want to post that picture of yourself in your underwear on Instagram?" As if to say, Of course it's fine with *me* if you do that, because personal boundaries are so late 1990s, but someone way less cool, who *doesn't* use Postmates to get their groceries delivered, might think it's just a wee bit of an overshare.

Old Lady Jackson isn't judgmental; she's just worried about you, and wonders about things like your nose ring (doesn't that hurt? And how can you possibly keep it clean?) and that sixth tattoo you got (isn't five enough?). But not me—no sirree, I'm proud of you for expressing yourself!

One morning in the *Gilmore Girls* makeup trailer (during the first series) I was prattling on to Alexis about the possibility of getting a tattoo and the exciting potential of designing it myself, because, I explained, that's where the real fun was, the real *artistry*. I could just picture my new tattooed life: I'd be out at some cool club or bar (assuming that along with my new tattoo I had also started going to cool clubs and bars for the first time ever), and some hot dude in a biker jacket would catch my eye and appreciatively check me out, and what better conversation opener, what more sure path to lifelong happiness and true bliss, than "Cool tat. Did you design that yourself?"

After I went on and on about my fantasy post-tattoo life for a while, Alexis smiled and gently said, "So, what would you get? A shamrock?"

Um, no. I mean, what? NO. A sham—? Please, that's just SILLY! Why would you think I'd get something as predictable as a sham—OH DEAR HOW EMBARRASSING YOU'RE RIGHT. I'M A CLICHÉ OF A SOMEWHAT IRISH PERSON. But hey, it's not like I was going to put it on my ankle, so at least there's—OH FINE OKAY YES THAT'S EXACTLY WHERE I WAS GOING TO PUT IT.

After my embarrassment faded, I realized I didn't want a tattoo anymore. Why? Because through her (more mature) eyes I suddenly saw the inherent futility of it. All at once, it was like I'd done it already, experienced a brief thrill, lived with it for a couple of years, and eventually woke up one day and felt like, huh, what a weird thing that was for me to do.

Sometimes the idea of doing something is the most fun part, and after you go through with it, you feel deflated because you realize you're back to looking for the next thrill. Often, waiting reveals the truth about something, and not responding to your every impulse can save you the heartache of waking up in the morning with a sense of regret after having impulsively texted that guy at 2:00 a.m. because you just *had* to tell him about the funny skit you just watched on SNL, and it's not like you want to date him or anything, and you'd only had one glass of wine, or was it two? But in any case he was probably up anyway! *Don't press send,* Old Lady Jackson is fond of counseling. *Just wait a beat.*

Talking about getting a tattoo was, I realized, a perfect case of life being about the journey and not the destination. And I felt relieved to have saved myself from reaching my destination with a lot of tattoos on my upper butt area that I'd then changed my mind about.

One of the best things about Old Lady Jackson is that when you *don't* take her advice (Miles and Mae have approximately seven thousand piercings between them, and exactly 152 tattoos each), it's fine with me! She's no fun, but I still am!

Old Lady Jackson is concerned about you in other ways too, but I think you're doing great! OLJ is (obviously overly) worried about things like that dating app that wants you to have your location services on *all the time* (how is that possibly safe?) and the fact that all you ate yesterday were liquids that came in mason jars from that juice place on the corner (really? No solid foods at all?). OLJ doesn't love it when that guy texts you at eleven o'clock on a Friday night after you haven't heard from him all week and wants you to "hang out," and you do. She's worried that you aren't being treated as well as you deserve, and while she understands that "things are different now," surely there have to still be people out there with better manners and an ability to make plans with you at least a day or two ahead of time?

Old Lady Jackson is also very worried about the alarming number of young people she's heard are being prescribed Adderall so that they can "focus better at school or work." In OLJ's day, they called the feeling of not wanting to sit in the library for hours the "feeling of not wanting to sit in the library for hours." And it wasn't considered a medical condition to be bored or distracted at work; it was just part of the reality of work.

A while ago I saw a young family in the airport, a couple with their young toddler, who was happily sitting in her carrying chair thing. All three were looking down, scrolling through their phones with glassy eyes, not speaking to one another. We see this a lot, of course, but this was the first time it really occurred to me how different things are now than when I grew up. I didn't have a mobile phone until I was in my late twenties. My fourteen-year-old godson just got one not too long ago. But the next generation, like this baby in the airport, will never know what life is like without a device. This raises a couple of questions: What does the future hold for this baby? And can she already beat me at Candy Crush?

We can all agree that airports are the worst, and a tough place to entertain a fussing baby. And presumably the parents were doing something important and would return their attention to each other and their baby in a moment. Probably the baby was sitting there learning to speak Mandarin or monitoring her stock portfolio. Even so, there's a checked-out, drugged sort of look we get when on our phones that's different from the look we get when reading a book, or even just staring into space. I get that look too, and when I catch my own reflection, it gives me a chill. It's like Gollum's face just before he drops his Precious in the water.

The people I know who use social media and dating apps

do so because they're trying to connect, stay in touch, and in some cases find someone to go out with or maybe even to fall in love and start a family with. In fact, this family in the airport was quite possibly *formed* by these advances in technology, and now, thanks to the wondrous connectivity to which we all have access, they had finally achieved their dream of finding each other—but they were still sitting in the airport scrolling through their phones. And this is just the beginning. Where will we go from here?

When my sister meets her work friends for dinner—a group of super-high-level New York business types—they sometimes do the following: everyone places their cellphone in the center of the dinner table, and the first one who can't take it anymore and goes to reach for their phone has to pay the bill. Fun! When I'm driving somewhere, I've started to put my purse in the trunk of the car to prevent myself from checking my phone at a stoplight. I think games like this are necessary until we figure out how else to resist the temptation to click on important breaking news stories while driving, like "Ten Cats with Surprisingly Human Faces!"

Or rather, *I* think it's all probably fine! Let's make a date to see each other and then spend twenty minutes scrolling through hundreds of photos looking for that one we just can't find! Let's not wonder about one single solitary thing when we can just Google it over appetizers! Let's leave our phones out on the table "in case of emergency," but respond to all the non-emergency texts anyway! It's just what people do! I'm totally okay with it! It's that crazy Old Lady Jackson who thinks it's weird, and she wrote you a letter on *actual paper* to give you her thoughts:

My Dearies:

I miss car keys. Those unattractive fob blobs they use now don't hang well on my key chain, and my gentleman friend is always forgetting to give them to the valet. What, you think Old Lady Jackson doesn't have the occasional suitor to escort her to a nice sushi dinner once in a while?

Please, please, sit down. No, not there, dear, that's for company. Have a cookie, you're too thin. Is it cold in here? What was that? Speak up, dear. I won't keep you long, I know you're busy. Let me tell you a story. One day, that horrible Marion from next door "invited" me to one of those group on-line thingies where we keep track of our steps and see who has the most—you know those? You do. Of course you do. Well, for a few weeks, I participated, and I thought it was the most wonderful thing. Such a sense of accomplishment at day's end! So I started counting absolutely everything, and got all these wonderful apps: I counted not just how many steps I took, but also how many hours I slept, how many calories I ate, how many followers I had on Facebook, what the weather was like in Hawaii, how my retirement stocks were doing. I got a countdown app to remind me how many days I had left to shop for my nephew's birthday. I got an app to track the constellations in the sky, an app to record how much money I spend at Starbucks, an app to remind me to water my plants, another that reminds me when to order more contact lenses, and one that tells me how many times I've listened to Doris

Day sing "Que Sera Sera" this week. Isn't progress wonderful? I got an app to read what everyone thinks of restaurants too. This one was confusing to me, because it seems every single restaurant in the country is just horrible. But anyway, I especially loved the steps app because I could look at the thingie marker, and if Marion was getting ahead of me, it would make me jump out of my chair and wave my arms around to get my count higher. I beat her so many days that I could almost forget all the times she hid my trash bins and stole my Sunday paper. Bliss.

Then my gentleman friend and I were home one night drinking prune juice with vodka and binge-watching <u>The Waltons</u>, and apparently I was getting up to check my phone more times than you can say "Good night, Jim-Bob." Finally my gentleman friend paused the VHS tape right on John-Boy's face and asked me what it was that was distracting me. And I told him it wasn't at all that I was distracted; I was just excited by all the wonderful new information that was coming in, and did he want to see the weather in Hawaii or join our step club too? No, he said, he didn't. And then he asked me a question. "Why?" he said. What was I going to do with all this information? Why keep track of so many things? And why did I keep marching around the living room waving my arms over my head? What did it all mean at the end of a day, or the end of a life, for that matter? (When you're our age you think about these things,

dear, but don't worry yourself about it just now—you're
still younger than you think.)

Anyway, everything suddenly went topsy-turvy and I had
to sit back down on the davenport. Have another cookie while
they're warm, won't you? My story is almost over. I had to sit
down, because I suddenly realized what a waste of time it all
was. I take my walk every morning rain or shine—who cares if
Marion goes a little farther? I water my plants when the soil
looks dry, and I haven't forgotten my nephew's birthday once
ever. In fact, I started to think about my nephew and all the
time he uses that phone, always checking for likes on that
Instacart. It's good to be bored in the car, I always tell him.
Spend some time with just yourself and your thoughts and
nothing to do. How else will you learn who you are?

I'm worried about your posture, dear. I'm concerned that
it comes from all the looking down. What with your phone
and the Xbox and the taxi TV and that music player you
wear on your arm and the headphones that look like donuts
on your ears, doesn't it make life so much smaller? If absolutely everything important is only happening on such a small
screen, isn't that a shame? Especially when the world is so
overwhelmingly large and surprising? Are you missing too
much? You can't imagine it now, but you'll look like me one
day, even though you'll feel just the same as you do now. You'll
catch a glimpse of yourself in the mirror and think how quickly
it's all gone, and I wonder if all the time you used watching

those families whose lives are filmed for the television, and making those cartoons of yourselves with panting dog tongues, and chasing after that terrible Pokémon fellow . . . well, will it feel like time well spent? "Here lies Ms. Jackson, she took more steps than the other old biddies on her road"—is that the best I can leave behind? Is it all just designed to keep us looking down, or to give us the illusion that we have some sort of control over our chaotic lives?

Will you do me a small favor, dears, and look up? Especially you New Yorkers and Londoners and other city dwellers who cross all those busy streets. How else will you take in the majesty of the buildings that have stood there for hundreds of years? How else will you run into an acquaintance on the street who might turn into a friend or a lover or even just recommend a good restaurant that no one has complained about on that app yet? If you never look out the window of the subway car, how will you see the boats gliding by on the East River, or have an idea that only you could have? Just look up for no reason, just for a moment here and there, or maybe for an entire day once in a while. Let the likes go unchecked and the quality of sleep go unnoticed. Que sera sera, my dears—whatever will be will be, whether we're tracking it on our GPS devices or not.

Look up! Look up! What you see might surprise you.

Love,

Old Lady Jackson

What It Was Like, Part Two

. . . .

Spoiler alert! The below contains plot and casting mentions, and some general information you may not want to have until after you've seen the new episodes. If you haven't watched *Gilmore Girls: A Year in the Life* yet, you might want to skip this part until you have.

Years from now, long after the *Downton Abbey* reboot (Matthew lives!), the *Six Feet Under* reboot (literally *The Walking Dead!*), and the reboot of the *Fuller House* reboot (don't be rude. Cut. It. Out. All over again!), I'll still be trying to explain what it was like to return to *Gilmore Girls*. That was the first question I got when the show was announced, and the one I've been asked most frequently ever since. It's also a question I don't feel I've quite answered satisfactorily. So far,

I've just stuttered and stammered and tried to find something to compare it to.

"It's like getting a chance to go to college all over again, but this time you know what classes to take, and you know how to really appreciate all the, uh, classes, and the people, and, uh . . ."

No, that's not what it was like.

"It's like, if you got back together with an old boyfriend, but now there were only the good parts about him, without all the stuff that bugged you, and you got to fall in love all over again, without making any of the mistakes you made when you, uh . . ."

No, that's not it either.

"It's like if you were diagnosed with a disease, but then the doctors realized they'd made a mistake and you were actually okay, so you experienced the feeling of enjoying every day that much more, because suddenly you'd been reminded how precious the days were, and you were even more thankful to have them because you'd been faced with the reality of how rare they actually are, when before you'd taken the days for granted and thought you were sick but you're not, and . . ."

Uh, no.

I have an old email from Amy from December 2014, where she mentions the possibility of taking a pitch out to some streaming services. That must mean that we'd already had our lunch at the Greek restaurant in Los Angeles where she first told me some of her ideas and started sketching out the early plotlines. Inspired by the British series *Sherlock,* which has no yearly set number of episodes but instead does anywhere from one to four specials, she envisioned four mini-movies that would run about ninety minutes each.

At that lunch, she asked if I'd read the Marie Kondo book *The Life-Changing Magic of Tidying Up.* Yes, I had, I replied. She also kept asking me if I'd read *Wild* and/or seen the movie. Yes to both, I told her, and why was she asking? We hadn't seen each other in a while and the reality of getting back together to do the show again seemed so far away, which meant we kept getting distracted and going off on tangents and she never really answered me about either. What she was mainly there to ask me was, if it was possible to somehow put this thing together, would I be interested?

Why, yes—yes, I would be.

A few months later, in early spring of 2015, Amy and Dan felt we were inching closer to the reality of making the show at Netflix, but we were still too far away to make any formal announcement. Warner Brothers and Netflix had to agree to a deal first, and then Amy and Dan would go in and pitch the story ideas, or was it the other way around? Would it be better to pitch the ideas first, then see if everyone could make a deal? This was all new territory. The two entities would be paying for the show, and they had to make nice with each other first, and that process was complicated. The existence of streaming was new, rebooting a show on a different network was new, and turning a show that once had been an hour long minus time for commercials into uninterrupted ninety-minute movies was new. And notice that no one was even talking about the actors yet. This could all take a while. "The *Green Eggs and Ham* deal took eighteen months," Amy told me. Eighteen months? Also, they're making *Green Eggs and Ham* into a movie? Anyway, I knew we didn't have that much time, in part because of the back lot.

The back lot. Oy.

You've heard of the town of Stars Hollow? Well, I'm here to tell you, it is real. It's a wonderful, happy place with cheerful neighbors, ballerinas taking classes at Miss Patty's, and a seasonal festival of some sort happening in the town square. It's a place where the coffee flows freely, junk food has no calories, and Kirk has somehow found yet another job. There, the town meeting might be in session (although I'm usually late for it), with Taylor Doose presiding, and outside, near the gazebo, there could be a hay bale maze set up for your enjoyment. It's a place where, on one special day every year, I smell snow. If that's where you'd like to leave your understanding of our beloved town, please skip the next paragraph.

Because sometimes it's also a place in Los Angeles on the Warner Brothers lot, where other people from other shows come to visit, and sometimes they stay for a while— occasionally for years. Shockingly, it turned out that no one had reserved that spot for us indefinitely and held it frozen in time in the event of our triumphant return. Lots of other shows needed the back lot around the same dates we needed it, so we'd been given a very narrow time frame in which to use it. Obviously, when you're returning to Stars Hollow, you have to have an actual Stars Hollow. But the reality of the scheduling was that if we couldn't find a way to start filming by February 2016, basically we wouldn't be filming at all.

In March 2015, with everything still very much up in the air, we were invited to the ATX Festival in Austin, Texas, for a

Gilmore Girls reunion. In my emails with Amy from that time, we discussed where to stay in Austin (the St. Cecilia), our shared eye doctor (Dr. Sacks), and theater (*Hand of God*—so good! And no, even back then you couldn't get *Hamilton* tickets). We also discussed the many rumors that were flying around. I heard the deal was getting close. I heard the deal was falling apart. Scott Patterson went on a podcast and mentioned there were "talks," which had basically been true since the day the show ended in 2007, but the comment caught fire and people thought he knew more than he was saying, when in fact none of us did. A few weeks after the festival I got a call from my agent saying that he'd finally heard Netflix had committed to making eight to ten episodes of our show. Great news! I emailed Amy, who said she'd heard no such thing.

In the meantime, Amy's mysterious questions continued. She asked me if I knew fellow Barnard alum Jeanine Tesori, and I said I didn't, but I loved her musical *Fun Home* with all my heart. Amy told me she was having back trouble and wondered if I'd ever had back trouble. She asked me if, on the old show, I remembered asking her to write the longest monologue that had ever been done on TV. Our scripts back then had averaged eighty-five pages when most one-hour shows are under fifty pages, but still, I wanted more!

Anyway, there were many emails going back and forth. We kept trying to meet for drinks, but plans kept moving (I forgot I had tickets to *Fish in the Dark* and other New York City scheduling problems), and I started getting confused as to which of her inquiries was regarding real life and which might be potential *Gilmore* plotlines. Does Lorelai deliver a long monologue about straining her back while listening to the works of Jeanine Tesori as she cleans out her closet wearing hiking boots? I wasn't sure.

Then one day, out of the blue, there was a press release that said Netflix would indeed carry the new episodes—four 90-minute movies. This was exciting, but news to practically everyone. Alexis, Kelly, Scott, and I had been involved in these casual conversations for months, and I'd had all those mysterious questions from Amy, of course, but suddenly it was real. Or, more accurately, suddenly Warner Brothers and Netflix had been able to make a real deal with each other to make movies that needed to start filming in under two months, and which had no sets built and zero actors formally attached. Fun! Sean Gunn posted a picture of himself on Twitter next to the announcement on his computer. He looked completely surprised, because he was. Amy and I spoke on the phone, and I congratulated her—er, us? But weeks after you were already excited about watching it, and I was being congratulated on being in it, no one had yet called me about actually doing it. Plus I was in Atlanta by then, filming the movie *Middle School,* which had months left to go, and as far as I could tell, the filming schedules totally conflicted. Um, was anyone else worried about this? It seemed no one was.

Finally one day the phone rang.

Deal making in Hollywood is a fun and straightforward process where everyone puts their cards on the table and then proceeds, like proper ladies and gentlemen, to respectfully agree to terms and sums of money that are fair to both sides . . . is a sentence that has never before been written.

Let me attempt to explain how it really happens.

Negotiating in Hollywood is like dating a horrible guy

whom you have to keep seeing because he is in charge of your paycheck. In order to get your money from him, you will have to put up with a lot of crap and pretend to enjoy it. Once he pays you, you can break up with him, but only until the next time you need him, at which time you'll have to pretend to be in love with him all over again and act as if you have no memory of the past. Paycheck Boyfriend does not return your phone calls, or else calls you only at weird times when he knows you can't talk. He compares you to other, hotter girls he's dated and finds you lacking, dismisses your past accomplishments, and makes sure you know he has twenty-five other people he can call to go to dinner with him. You have earned this treatment by being very successful! Aren't you lucky! The problem is that if Paycheck Boyfriend treats you better, you might want him to pay you more, and he really, really, really doesn't want to do that. It's not entirely Paycheck Boyfriend's fault either, because he himself has a Corporate Paycheck Boyfriend who is treating him even worse, who cares mostly about how the stock of whatever company owns the studio is doing, and doesn't understand why drones can't star in TV shows instead of actors, since they are just as talented but have less body fat. "Why can't we do a show starring the self-driving Google car?" CPB is fond of asking.

It seems insane to me now, but the truth is that up until about a week before filming started, the reality of making the show was still very much up in the air. So many pieces had to come together, so many people's schedules had to align. Some actors weren't approached at all until after filming had actually started, because the days and weeks leading up to that first day were so chaotic, plus we have a cast that numbers in the hundreds. Among other oddities, this meant I had almost no time to prepare or to process the fact that I was going back to the character I'd loved so much. Maybe that's why so much of the show had such a surreal quality. But in the beginning, I was just relieved not to be negotiating anymore. To let you all know it was really happening, I tweeted this photo:

The caption read: "I can now confirm: it's time for me, and this jacket I stole in 2007, to return to work." By the way, stealing is wrong! (Unless it's fun material for your book. Then it's okay.)

You'd think that all those years of being asked about the possibility of making a movie would have prepared me for finally doing one. Or four. But we'd spent seven years without a real possibility, over a year with only a vague one, and then a flurry of a few weeks in which major decisions had to be made and suddenly everything was a go. Even though I knew it was real, in a way, I don't know if my brain ever quite caught up to the reality of what was happening. I still sort of can't believe it happened. It happened, right? I have honestly never had an experience like it.

For starters, I was very, very emotional the whole time. I don't usually cry easily, but throughout the days and months of filming, I welled up a lot. I've told the story before about how Alexis was so green when we first started, and our walk-and-talks so lengthy and complex, that I'd sometimes put my arm through hers to help guide her to our mark. But the first day we returned to Lorelai's house it was me who reached for her arm for support—I was so overwhelmed that I felt a little shaky.

And then there was the day I walked onto the grand Gilmore house stage for the first time. It wasn't just emotional because it had been re-created. It was also genuinely sad because Ed Herrmann had passed away the previous winter. You know how some people have such a big presence they just fill up a room? You might enter, and before you even see them you know they're there? That was Ed. His presence was as tall and warm as he was. So his absence had a feeling too—the room was entirely different without his booming voice and easy laugh. Kelly spoke to him that first day on set. "Ed? We know you're here. We miss you," she said, and everyone choked up.

Those tears made sense. But some of my other teary reactions were just bizarre. For example, when Chris Eigeman, a dear friend, came to do his cameo, we sat down for a casual rehearsal, and as we started to read through our scene, I could not manage to get through my first line: "Why, Jason Stiles, as I live and breathe." Normally, saying hello to someone in the beginning of a scene is not the emotional high point for the character or the actor. I was just so happy to see him again. My normal state of happy-to-see-someone does not usually involve tears, but on this show tissues were being handed to me a lot.

In another scene, I had trouble getting through the simple sentence "My name is Lorelai Gilmore, and I'm from a little town in Connecticut." All I'm doing in that scene is giving some strangers basic information. Still, for some reason, tears. I guess I was overwhelmingly happy to get to say her name again.

For the reboot, all the sets had to be reconstructed, which also contributed to the surreal quality. No one had saved any set pieces from the old show, because why would they have? Netflix didn't exist when the show ended, and no one had had any concrete reason to believe we'd be back in the Gilmore house or Luke's diner or Stars Hollow ever again. There was no gazebo on the back lot anymore—they had to build one. There were no precise measurements of the rooms either, so while sets were reconstructed as closely as possible, in most cases the measurements were slightly off. This added to the eerie quality of being back: in the Gilmore house, for example, the foyer was completely familiar, yet just a little bit larger than it was in the original. Everything was the same yet brand-new. I noticed the slight changes because I knew these spaces as intimately as if it were a real house I'd actually lived in for years.

We were back on the Warner Brothers lot, as we had been the first time around, but all the stages that housed our sets were in different places. It was a constant surprise to walk out of Lorelai's house and run into friends who work on the *Ellen* show, because previously we hadn't been anywhere near *Ellen*. But on the other hand, because certain sets were so familiar, I'd sometimes lose track of where I was in time— for several fleeting moments every day, I'd think I was still doing the old show, until something from the present would remind me that time had passed.

Then there was El Niño. Given how tight our time was on the back lot, we couldn't afford to lose any days there. But huge storms were predicted. And lots of rain. There aren't many cloudy days in a town like Stars Hollow, so we worried. And we waited. But not only did it not storm, the weather played its part during the seasonal episodes as though it too had been cast in the show. When we were filming "Summer" it was balmy, "Fall" had a bit of crisp in the air, in "Spring" breezes lifted us up, and during "Winter" we had an unseasonable chill. For usually predictable Southern California, this was nothing short of magical. And the predicted El Niño storms? They didn't happen.

Through it all, the emotion I felt most was gratitude. I treasured every experience and savored every scene in a way that was different from when I did the original show. Partially this had to do with being in a different place personally and professionally. I wasn't new to the business anymore, and I had a much more acute sense of how lucky I was to be part of this cast and crew. I treasured the chance to speak words written by the Palladinos once more. And I now understood in greater depth how rare it was to have had the opportunity to be part of something this special in the first place. In the flurry of the first incarnation it was hard to have much perspective. This time I was thankful for every single day.

We were also buoyed by the enthusiasm we felt from all of you. Normally, when actors start a new show, we have no idea if what we're doing will work, or if people will like it. To know we were making something that at least some people were already very excited about seeing was a thrilling novelty, and your support was a big part of what made every day feel special. Thank you so much for that. After all those years of having no answer when asked by you (and Mike Ausiello!) about the possibility of a *Gilmore Girls* movie, finally I had something to say. And that we'd landed at Netflix was an honor too. Executives usually walk around looking jumpy, but these Netflix and Warner Brothers execs were happy and smiling throughout it all. "We knew it was big, but we had no idea it was *this* big," they said. Everyone was excited and proud.

So, what was it like? The truth is, it was so many things at once that there is no short way to describe it, no sound bite that does it justice. But I did keep a diary of sorts (which I wish I'd done the first time around), to try to cut through how overwhelming much of it was and to have a record I could look back on when it was done, to see if that could help me process the whole experience.

Here are just a few of the most memorable days of filming *Gilmore Girls: A Year in the Life.*

TUESDAY, FEBRUARY 2, 2016

It's the first day of filming. As I said, we had very little time between "Are we doing this?" and "Wow, we're doing this!" Plus I was on location in Atlanta until less than a week before *Gilmore Girls* filming was supposed to start. So while normally I'd have had a bunch of fittings with Brenda, the costume designer, and we'd have planned at least the early round of outfits, in this case we had time for just one fitting and had chosen only a handful of looks.

The morning is a bit of a scramble, as they usually are. The first scene we're filming is not the first scene you see, but it is a piece of the opening sequence, so basically I'm choosing the outfit for the first time you see Lorelai, and I keep fussing over what it should be. Whatever we chose already just doesn't seem right to me today for some reason, so I ask for more choices. "Just bring a bunch of tops and let me mess around a little," I say to Cesha, my on-set dresser. Cesha and I worked together for all seven years on the first show, so she knows what that means. She loads up a rolling rack with a ton of stuff. I keep trying things on and taking them off—nothing feels right. A knock on my door tells me the cameras are ready, so I pull a blue blouse off its hanger—when in doubt, blue! It's a little big, so Cesha pins it in the back for me. Then I jump on my bicycle and speed to set.

I like to have a bike to ride to and from set, rather than take the van they usually provide. Sometimes those short moments in between setups are the only ones I have to myself during a long day, and I like to get even that short burst of exercise. The bicycle I'm using is brand-new—a light green bike that was the wrap gift from *Parenthood*. Our boss, Jason Katims, gave one to every member of the cast and crew. Nice! The bikes all came with license plates that say BRAVERMAN. I looked at the license plate on the first day and wondered if I should take it off—would I get confused and start wondering where Hank was? But I decided it was nice to bring a little Sarah along for the ride.

I pedal to set and get touched up. Right before we start rolling, I feel an itch on the back of my neck. Maybe one of the safety pins Cesha used to pin the shirt is poking through? Cesha realizes that in my haste to get dressed I didn't take the tags out. She snips them off, and we start the scene.

The first day is full of happy smiling faces. One of my favorites to see back is George, our dialogue coach. After we run lines, he talks about last night's *American Idol* and reminds me how we used to love dishing about it back in the day. I remember being awed by Kelly Clarkson then (whom I've since been lucky enough to meet). We talk about how funny and perfect it is that *AI* is in its final season, and now we'll get a chance to chat about the contestants again one last time. The day goes smoothly, and it's truly bizarre how easy it is to get back in the groove I left behind all those years ago.

At the end of the day, Cesha knocks on my trailer door. She has a funny look on her face. "I want to show you something," she says. "I swear I didn't see this before."

She hands me a small piece of cardboard, and for a moment it doesn't quite compute. "What is this?" I ask her.

"It's the tag from the shirt you wore this morning," she says. "I cut it off earlier, but I didn't look at it until just now."

I glance at the tag again, and this time I gasp. I wouldn't believe it if I hadn't seen it, and neither would you, so here it is:

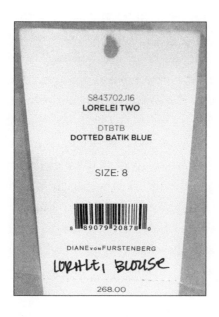

Can you believe it? Okay, the spelling of the name is one letter off. But the shirt has a name. And it's *my character's name.* And it's not just called "The Lorelei," which would be coincidence enough, but it's called "The Lorelei *Two*"! And it's our very first day, and it's the *second time* I'm playing Lorelai! And it's—okay, okay, you get it. Cesha and I look at each other, eyes wide. I wonder if I've fallen into some sort of magical fairy omen land. At the very least, I take it as an incredible sign of good things to come. I tape it up on the wall over the sink in my trailer, to remind me every day that strange and wonderful magic might be in store.

WEDNESDAY, FEBRUARY 10

Yanic and I have a scene at the Dragonfly where he's upset that all the A-list actors in town to shoot a movie are staying at a rival inn and the Dragonfly is stuck with the B-list actors. It culminates with him moaning, "We will never bag Jennifer Lawrence, and what's the point of living if you can't bag Jennifer Lawrence!" Yanic's Michel has always been a terrific comedic character, but in this series he gets to really shine, and we had a wonderful time in our scenes together.

Then Paul Anka (the person, not the dog) arrives, to be in Lorelai's anxiety dream. He (the person, not the dog) is hilarious and professional, and he looks like a million bucks. Although we've worked together before, I get weirdly shy around him and out of nowhere ask him how many kids he has. Like, we weren't talking about kids or anything related to them. He probably just said he had a great pasta at lunch, and I replied, "How many kids do you have?" What a weirdo.

THURSDAY, FEBRUARY 11

President Obama is a guest on *The Ellen DeGeneres Show* today, and the lot is in a security tizzy. I'm called in earlier than needed "in case they jam all the cellphones." Um, they can do that? We're shooting the scene where Lorelai tells Luke she's going away to "do *Wild*" (the book, not the movie). I say the line "I know" thirteen times, but it's an oddly emotional scene—the beginning of a big journey for Luke and Lorelai.

FRIDAY, FEBRUARY 12

Dax Shepard is in the hair and makeup trailer! Worlds collide. He's getting a haircut from one of the stylists he knows who's working with us, and drinking a green juice in preparation for starring in *CHiPs*, which he also wrote and directed. Not only is he obviously some sort of genius, but his already non-existent body fat has gone down to the level of Mount Everest's. What's that? Mountains don't have body fat? Neither does Dax Shepard. He gives me one of his signature full-body-contact hugs. Nice way to start the day!

TUESDAY, FEBRUARY 16

Throughout the shoot, for general security and to prevent being seen by all of you industrious Internet cuties, our scripts and sides (the mini-scripts of the day's work) are all watermarked with our names on them. That way, if something leaks, they know who's to blame. The sides are numbered as well, to keep track of how many copies are circulating. I tend to lose things on set to a ridiculous degree: glasses, purses, phones. I'm always stashing things behind a cushion somewhere and then forgetting where I put them. I lose my sides ten times a day and am always borrowing someone else's. So, as a joke, even if I'm only on my first sides of the day, they're marked LG #4, as if I've already lost three before we've even started. Hahahahaha! I'll get you, AD staff!

Eddy, my agent, comes to visit. Well, let's be honest—he came to visit his other client on the lot, World Pro Wrestling champion Ellen DeGeneres. At least that's what she does for a living in *my* book! She can't cut to commercial here! I'm drunk with power! Eddy tells me he has "medium to high expectations" regarding the outcome of the show, which, in agent-speak, means . . . well, I'm pretty sure he just proposed marriage.

Sarah Ramos, who played my niece on *Parenthood,* also comes to visit today. I put her in the background of one of the scenes. Can you spot her?

My regular hair magician, Anne Morgan, is out for the day, and one of my favorite hair dudes, Jonathan Hanousek, is playing sub. He always knows the latest in top-secret Hollywood secrets, and today he tells me about software being developed for a camera that detects eye and mouth movement but softens everything else on a person's face into a pleasingly smooth facelike blob. It's designed to help older actors look younger, I guess? Wow, weird—and where do I apply for this blob technology?

MONDAY, FEBRUARY 22

Sutton Foster is in town. SUTTON FOSTER IS IN TOWN. She's just here for fittings and rehearsal, but will be back in a few weeks to shoot her scenes.

I feel like we could play sisters in something. Do you?

WEDNESDAY, FEBRUARY 24

Right around now I realize that I don't know, and have never known, what the last four words of the show are. This may seem insane given how excited everyone apparently is to finally learn them. Even worse, I didn't even know the last four words were a "thing." I don't know how it's possible that I missed this information. Amy and I just never talked about it for some reason, and Old Lady Jackson doesn't know her way 'round the old Tinternet too well, and somehow the whole hoopla missed me entirely, probably in no small part due to my insistence on using archaic words like "hoopla." When I tell her this at work, Amy tilts her head and looks at me like she thinks I'm kidding. "I never told you what they were?" she says. "Wow." She can't believe it. "Well, would you like to know them now, or do you want to wait until the day we have to film them?"

I have to admit, my heart starts pounding a little, and even though I didn't know until very recently that I've waited more than fifteen years for this information, I'm still not sure I'm ready for it yet. "Um . . . I don't know. Um, who says the four words?" I ask, stalling.

"You both do," she says, meaning me and Alexis. And for a moment I think I still don't want to know yet—I want to draw it out even more. Maybe I'll try to guess them instead? But my mind is a blank. It's too much pressure! Fans and Mike Ausiello, how did you handle the not knowing all these years?

"Okay, go ahead," I say. "Tell me." I'm, like, gasping for air. It's truly ridiculous how nervous I feel. Amy then tells me the last four words. She says them quickly. I blink back at her a few times, with no expression. Then I go suddenly calm. I realize I'm also holding my breath, like I'm getting the results of a bi-opsy. When I finally exhale, I think my reaction goes something like "Huh." And after that, it goes something like *"Really?"*

I'm actually still so paranoid given all the fuss over them that I'm not even going to say them here—maybe you know them by now, anyway? The words are wonderful, of course, and have a simple symmetry, which makes perfect sense within the origin of the story of *Gilmore Girls*. They are not, however, what I was expecting, because they are not what I would call the exact definition of a conclusion. As in they do not end the story we are telling as much as they introduce something that was not previously known. Which, to me, is not precisely an ending. To me, they are really more of a . . .

"Isn't that more of a *cliffhanger*?" I ask Amy.

But Amy doesn't answer me.

She just smiles.

Hmmmm.

FRIDAY, FEBRUARY 26

Unbelievably, the first "block" of the schedule is over. This means we're finished with one-third of our work. Gulp. It's flying by. Today we begin several days of scenes at Miss Patty's—a series of town hall meetings. One of my best friends, Sam Pancake (yes, that's his real name), is here, playing a new character named Donald. I'd always wanted him to come on the show before, but there was never anything he was exactly right for. Still, I'd asked Amy and Dan about him so many times over the years that when everything was finally happening for sure, I couldn't help trying again. I started to tell Amy that, as lucky as I already felt to be back, I was hoping for just one more thing.

"I know, I know," Amy said before I could finish. "We'll find a part for Sam."

Ha! You'd think that finally having that dream fulfilled would be enough. But I continued to try to jam friends and family in anywhere I could. My friend Clare Platt walks through town in "Fall," my godson Clyde passes me near the gazebo in "Winter," Mae and other surprise friends play key (or sometimes not so key) roles. If you were a loved one who came to visit, I wanted it on film.

MONDAY, FEBRUARY 29

All the table reads have been fantastic, but today is the first half of our last episode, and there's a special electricity in the room. Because we're in the middle of filming, the "Fall" table read is being broken into two. We'll read the first part today and the rest tomorrow. In the previous table reads Kelly has been reading her part over the phone from her home in New Jersey, but she's finally here in person. Seeing her is wonderful, but it makes me realize again how much I'm missing Ed. He would have loved this whole experience so much.

A word about "Fall": I couldn't read it for the longest time. It just so happened that we weren't filming any scenes from it in the first few weeks, so I could get away with it for a while. Amy kept asking if I'd read it yet, and I'd just giggle nervously. I'm not sure what was stopping me—maybe fear of it all being over, or fear that I'd be disappointed in how the show ended after all this time. But the day I finally sat down in my kitchen to read it is one I'll never forget. I cried from start to finish.

TUESDAY, MARCH 1

The second half of the table read for "Fall." David Sutcliffe is there even though he's shot his scene with Alexis already. It's so good to see him. We always had a special affection for each other, and I'm sad we didn't have any scenes together in the reboot. I ask him if he notices that this ending is not necessarily an ending—it's almost a cliffhanger. Right? I mean I'm right, right? I mention it again to Amy and Dan too, but they don't say anything. They just nod and smile.

I don't know if it's the longest monologue in the history of television, like Amy and I discussed back in the day, but the speech I have about Richard near the end of the episode is certainly the longest I've ever had as an actor. I also think it's a beautiful tribute by Amy both to Richard and to Ed. The whole episode is very emotional, and by the end of the table read everyone is a total wreck.

WEDNESDAY, MARCH 2

Our Netflix execs, Matt Thunell and Brian Wright, stop by and tell us the first seven seasons of the show will start streaming internationally in July. I wonder if Alexis and I will get to travel to faraway lands. . . .

Yanic has to talk about *The Sound of Music* in a scene at the Dragonfly today, and he asks me to describe it to him, since he's never seen it. He also wants me to pronounce *auf Wiedersehen* for him. It turns out German words in a French accent are adorable. Gary, who was my assistant for ten years, all through the entirety of the old show, visits. Gary had a cameo one of those years, but I'd love for him to have something more substantial this time. Another loved one to add to the list!

THURSDAY, MARCH 3

Scott and I have a big scene. During a break, I ask him if he's noticed that the ending is really more of a cliffhanger. He sort of shrugs. No one seems as bothered by this as I do.

Kelly Wolf, the real-life mom of Max from *Parenthood*, plays a real estate agent in a few scenes with Scott and Kelly today. Worlds collide again!

Amy and I discuss wanting to go to the Smokehouse to

have a martini and cheesy bread. Alexis and I talk about planning a dinner. None of us know it yet, but we won't have time for any of it until the entire shoot is over.

FRIDAY, MARCH 4

It's my first scene with Kelly, and our first day on the Gilmore house set together. In the show, Emily has commissioned a portrait of Richard, and as we enter the living room there's his face, ten feet tall. For a moment no one can speak. Then Kelly asks Ed to somehow make his presence known today by doing something big and loud. Later, during the scene, a key light goes out for no reason.

"Thanks, Ed," she says.

Tears.

THURSDAY, MARCH 10

When I first read the *Stars Hollow, the Musical* scenes in Dan Palladino's "Summer" episode, I thought, oh, those could be sort of fun. But when I tell you I could have watched Sutton Foster and Christian Borle perform them all day, I am not exaggerating. Dan and Amy wrote the lyrics, and the music is by Jeanine Tesori (*Fun Home, Shrek*). The songs are amazing and hilarious. I could hardly keep a straight face. I predict this mini-musical will go viral and be performed on college campuses everywhere.

Later in the day, Sutton's character sings a more serious song to me, a turning point when Lorelai realizes she needs to go on a journey. You'll be shocked and surprised to learn I cried through every single take. It was a privilege to get to be in scenes with these two.

WEDNESDAY, MARCH 16

It's my birthday, and my dad, stepmother Karen, sister Maggie, and brother-in-law Rick have come to town to visit set and celebrate. Morgan and Tania McComas, my makeup artist, decorate the hair and makeup trailer and shower me with treats, and everyone in the trailer shares some of the giant banana pudding from Magnolia Bakery. These ladies have taken extra-special care of me during our run, and I'm grateful to them.

My father, who recently retired, thinks it's a funny idea to take a picture in front of the Stars Hollow Pretty Pastures retirement home to try to trick his friends into thinking he's moving there. Ha!

THURSDAY, MARCH 17

It's our last day of filming *Stars Hollow, the Musical* at Miss Patty's, and the last day of work for Carole King, who's been on set for the last few days reprising her role as Sophie. It's also the last day for my dear Sam. After a long day of filming, it's a wrap, and everyone starts to disperse. Carole is petite and quiet, a sensitive observer. But today she stands up and walks with purpose through the crowd and over to the piano. Her hands hover over the keys, and she calls out in her distinctively raspy voice: "Anyone want to hear a song?" Everyone freezes. A few phones go up. "Can we film it?" someone asks.

Carole smiles and thinks for a moment, then cheerfully says, "Nope!" The phones go down. Word goes out over the walkies. Crew members squeeze into the already crowded room, a hush descends, and Carole starts to play.

It is simply incredible.

Because no one is worrying about recording it, we all get to truly experience this intimate mini-concert. (Old Lady Jackson would be proud.) I look around the room and see the faces of so many people I love. They're all lit up. Carole sings "I Feel the Earth Move" and encourages us to join in, which we do, singing softly, swaying to the beat. At the end, applause fills the room. It goes on and on. She brings the house down. Then people start chattering, excited about what they've just seen. We think it's over. But: "One more!" Carole says. And then she starts to play "You've Got a Friend." The faces, all the faces: Sally, Biff, Rose, my dear, dear Sam. My AD Eric, who came over from *Parenthood*. Dan, Amy. Old friends and new. You've never seen such happy faces. When I catch Amy's eye, I can guess what my own face might look like: red and puffy with tears streaming down. We smile at each other, shake our heads as if to say: *I still can't believe it. Can you believe it? We made it! We're here! These strange and wonderful days are actually happening!*

And just then Carole gets to the part of the song I sort of forgot was coming, even though I've heard it a million times: "Winter, spring, summer, or fall, all you've got to do is call . . ."

I'm gone. Destroyed. A sniffling mess.

Later, as everyone is filing out, Amy and Dan find me and tell me that what's funny is that Carole doesn't even know the episodes are named after her song, or that they're in that very order because of it. They haven't even asked her yet if they can use that song somewhere in the show, although they want to. It's just the song she chose to play. Another incredible co-incidence.

I nod and blink back more tears. At this point, I'm not even that surprised. I've come to accept this unique, magical time. Charmed days, and another funny miracle.

FRIDAY, MARCH 18

It's the night we're filming the last scene of the show, the final four words. Anyone who comes to set has to sign a confidentiality agreement. Alexis and I shoot the ending, and that's followed by these incredible sequences with dancers flitting by in gauzy skirts. Scott pushes me on a sort of rolling cart through a tunnel of greenery, and I feel like I'm flying, like I'm Alice in Wonderland.

Scott and I have one very brief dance move. It lasts a few seconds at most. But Marguerite, the choreographer, says she can tell I have some natural ability. I'm sure she just said it to be nice. But I still haven't stopped bragging about it around the house ever since.

MONDAY, MARCH 21

I wake up in the middle of the night thinking about coffee. Is Lorelai drinking enough coffee? Personally, I'm practically made of the stuff at this point, but I make a mental note to ensure she is too.

Mae comes to do her cameo, but she's very, very, ill. She

has a terrible stomach flu. So if our brief scene seems a bit off to you, it's because our main intention was to get through it before she needed the vomit bucket again. Hollywood! It's all glitz and glamour!

Michael Ausiello also has his cameo today. He sends me a nice note about it afterward, telling me how emotional it was to be there. I feel you, bro.

WEDNESDAY, MARCH 23

Today we're filming the opening shot of "Winter," and of the whole series. Even though we've been shooting for a while now, I'm so nervous I hardly slept. Overnight, the town has miraculously been decorated and covered in snow. I'm not sure what they make it out of, but I'm pretty sure I still have some on my Ugg boots from the first time we made the show. Alexis and I walk arm in arm through the town, as we've done so many times before. I'm all right in the morning, but a bit later I can barely get through the line "I smell snow." We've been at this for a while now, but I still can't seem to get a grip.

TUESDAY, APRIL 5

"Hey, is that the same bike as last time?" a random crew guy from another show calls out as I go whizzing by.

"New bike, same character!" I say. I'm having déjà vu, and so, apparently, are other people.

My editor, Jen Smith, visits, and is worried about the book deadline. She spends the day on set and sees how many hours I'm working, how short the writing time between set-ups is. "Do you think you're going to make it?" she asks. She looks very nervous. I feel bad. I wonder if we'll ever work together on a project where I'm not actively raising her blood pressure for months at a time. Let's be honest—probably not!

Melissa does *Ellen* and announces she'll be a part of *Gilmore Girls,* then comes to visit the set afterward. I haven't seen her in ages, but it's like no time has passed. She's wearing a gorgeous floral dress that she designed. Melissa has always been an incredible decorator with great taste, and we had fun comparing notes when furnishing our first houses, which were right down the street from each other. We all stand around chatting—Melissa and her husband, Ben, me and Yanic and Amy and Dan—until work finally calls us back. Just like old times.

Today's scenes are with Kelly, where Emily Gilmore has read *The Life-Changing Magic of Tidying Up* and has decided to get rid of almost everything in the house. There are Gilmore antiques strewn about on every surface. It's a funny scene on one level, but it's also about how Emily is struggling to move on, and Kelly is characteristically fantastic in it.

The *Entertainment Weekly* cover about the show isn't supposed to be out for another week, but we learn it's been leaked online. The publishers are shocked—the only other time they had a breach like this was when someone got hold of their *Star Wars* cover before publication. Nice company! Thanks, Internet hackers!

SATURDAY, APRIL 9

Mae surprises me by booking massages for us at our favorite place. Usually we have to book weeks in advance, and I ask her how she got us in with such short notice. She admits that she pretended to be my assistant. Apparently my assistant's name is Mindy, and she's "cordial but firm."

MONDAY, APRIL 11

Rachael Ray is here! She's a total doll and does a fantastic job in her scene.

TUESDAY, APRIL 19

Roy Choi is here! He's extremely nice, but I forgot to ask for a photo. He's an intense and smart guy and comes extremely well prepared for his scene. In between takes, he discusses the similarities between being a chef and acting, noting that both professions require individual precision while maintaining an awareness of the whole. Whoa.

During the scene about whether or not we should fire Roy, Yanic keeps saying "baloney" instead of "abalone," which cracks everyone up. Apparently he's never eaten either.

Gary. I still need to find a part for Gary.

The props man, Mike, has asked me every day this week what I would like to eat in the upcoming camping scene instead of the dehydrated meatballs that are scripted. He needs to make them ahead of time and make sure he has plenty on hand in case we do a lot of takes. Chocolate meringue balls? Coconut macaroon balls? Veggie burger balls? For some reason, I can't decide. "Can I tell you later?" I ask.

WEDNESDAY, APRIL 20

Mae and Alexis are cast in a reading together! Really, worlds, could you collide any more? I wish I could've been there to see the magic of my two most special ladies on a stage together!

FRIDAY, APRIL 22

We just heard that Prince died yesterday. Amy was a giant fan and saw him in concert many times, and everyone is generally depressed about the loss.

My high school yearbook from my senior year appears in the mail. The wife of a friend from high school found it in storage. I gave it to her now-husband to sign on the last day of school, and he forgot to return it to me. So that's how I can finally reveal to you my other longtime passion, one I've never before discussed: the time I spent dedicating my young life to Interbuilding Communications.

Um, huh? That's my high school boyfriend, Charlie, over my left shoulder, which may have had something to do with my involvement in this club, but I have zero memory of it

Interbuilding Communications: A. Brinsmade, L. Graham, C. Gregg, M. Maganias, B. Price, M. Shenk.

otherwise. I guess if you ever find yourself in northern Virginia and you're wondering whom to thank for how well all the buildings there seem to be getting along, well, that would be me and my bangin' sweater vest.

The props guy is back. He *really* needs to know what I would like to eat in the dehydrated meatball scene. Granola cluster balls? Turkey meatball bites? Actual dehydrated meatballs? I still can't decide! I ask if I can let him know later. He sighs.

SATURDAY, APRIL 23

From the first time I read the script for "Fall," where Lorelai goes off on a wilderness adventure, I knew that Peter had to play the role of Park Ranger. In some ways in real life, Peter *is* a park ranger, and doing something outdoorsy and nature-related for a living is definitely another way his life could have gone. Plus, the character appears late in the show and I thought it would be a fun surprise for you to see him. His ABC show, *The Catch,* very kindly cleared him to do it. But now it's two days before he's due to work with us and something has come up—they've lost a location for an important scene and have to do some switching around. Which means now they can't spare Peter for the whole day. Park Ranger is in two lengthy scenes, both in Malibu, which is easily an hour from anywhere else in Los Angeles. So we have to think fast! Maybe we can split the two scenes into two different roles? But who else can we call at this late date? *How can we pull this off?*

MONDAY, APRIL 25

We pulled it off! Thanks, Jason Ritter!

WEDNESDAY, APRIL 27

Someone casually mentions that today is our last day on the set of Lorelai's house. Wait, what? For the first time I realize we are really and truly near the end. Ten days left of filming. How did that happen? It occurs to me that I should take something from the set as a memento. For years journalists have asked whether I took anything from the set of the old show, which I didn't, since we had no idea at the time that our last day was our last day. My blue coat was something I went home in one day and sort of forgot about until it was time to come back. Besides, they always seem more interested in intentional hardcore theft anyway. I'm not sure at what point taking things from sets became a time-honored thespian tradition—I can't picture Ingrid Bergman stealing from the set of *Casablanca*. But I know I'll be asked, so I start looking for something. I text Alexis to see if she wants anything. She hasn't left for the day yet, and says she'll come down to the set and look too.

There is no stranger feeling than the two of us wandering around our house trying to find what we want to take. "Was this here before?" we keep asking each other. So much has been reconstructed, plus Lorelai's kitchen has been updated, so everything is sort of familiar, yet also new. Alexis takes a Yale banner down from the wall of Rory's room. I take a pink flamingo made of tin that hung on the wall in the kitchen. I had no particular connection to this flamingo, but I do now, because it will always be the story I'll tell about the thing I took. I also take a few framed photos and an apple-shaped magnet with Rory's face on it that says YOU'RE THE APPLE OF MY EYE. Alexis cracks open a split of champagne she's been saving, and Alexis, Amy, and I share a brief toast before going back to work. So long, Lorelai's house! It's sad to say goodbye, but at least this time I know it's our last day together. Although . . . does anyone else notice that the ending is really more of a cliffhanger?

THURSDAY, APRIL 28

The producers of *The Royal We,* which I'm supposed to be adapting right now, call to ask how the script is coming. I take a deep breath, put my most professional writer hat on, and call them back and say something like "La la la la la la, I can't hear you." Luckily, they're nice about it.

We find a part for Gary! He can play the docent in the whaling museum scene with Kelly. But the part shoots Monday and Gary is in New York. Can Gary get to L.A. by Monday? Gary is going to look into it.

MONDAY, MAY 2

Three delayed airplanes and one harried overnight journey later, Gary makes it from New York! After his scenes, we sit in my trailer, catch up, and talk about all the long days and late nights we shared for seven years. For some reason, reminiscing with him makes me realize, really for the first time, that we're almost done.

TUESDAY, MAY 10

It's the second-to-last day of work. Getting Melissa back was the final, and in some ways to me most important, piece of this puzzle. I can't tell you what a joy it was to be back in the kitchen as Lorelai with my best friend, Sookie. I'd missed Melissa terribly in real life too.

After work, Melissa and Yanic and I go out for a drink. We talk for hours, and I could have stayed for hours more, but I have to try to get some sleep. Tomorrow is our last day, and it's going to be a long one.

WEDNESDAY, MAY 11

The day we've all been waiting for is finally here! I'm not just talking about our final day of work—it's also the day I must answer the deep philosophical question this book's been asking, which is what will I eat instead of dehydrated meatballs? I think you'll be relieved to know I went with coconut chocolate balls. Finally, with this global political issue settled, you can return to your lives!

Alexis and I spend most of the day shooting a scene that takes place in a New York City hotel room. Rory comes back after having a fling and worries it was a mistake. Lorelai tries to counsel her. Alexis plays the scene with a perfect blend of panic and humor. The rest of our sets have been taken down already—this is the only one left—and as we finish up the scene, I'm already feeling sad. I'm going to miss Alexis so much, as well as the special connection we share.

The last shot of the night, and of the show, is a re-creation of a sort-of tunnel that Lorelai, Luke, and Rory go through, a short pickup of a shot that we started outside at night but didn't have time to finish on the back lot many weeks ago. It will make sense when you see the show, but it's part of a sequence that's sort of magical; it's set to the Sam Phillips song "Reflecting Light," and has no dialogue. I can count on one hand the number of scenes I had over the years on *Gilmore Girls* that didn't have dialogue, which adds to the strangeness of it all. Some people have started to assemble near the monitor: members of our production staff, our ADs and their assistants, some folks from the office. There's nothing to see exactly, but I know they're gathering around us to say good-bye, to be there for the end, and there's an electricity in the air. We three pass silently together through this passageway five or six times.

And then, finally, that's a wrap.

I've shed so many tears over these weeks and months that while I'm very emotional, I'm also nearly dry-eyed—almost like I'm in shock. Amy and I hug. Scott and I hug. Dan and I hug. Alexis and I hug. We all stand around, a bit awkward, not exactly sure what to do next. We take some pictures, try-ing to capture a moment that's impossible to capture. In them, I look completely dazed.

Later, still dressed in the pajama bottoms I wore in the scene (and a top too, don't worry), I meet some cast and crew at the Smokehouse, our neighborhood haunt, and we talk for a bit and say thank you and look at each other, still a little dumbfounded. We did it! Right? I mean, we did it, didn't we? No one knew if it would ever happen, and we still almost can't believe it really did.

After a drink or two, I head back to my trailer to pack up a few more things before it gets too late, and I realize I can't find my blue coat. Did I leave it on set, like I always do? A call down to the stage tells us it's not there. The ADs get on the walkies. They've all seen this coat around me, or on me, or near me almost every day, so everyone knows exactly what they're looking for. Plus it's long and puffy and blue—it can't have gone far. But no one has seen it. When was the last time I had it? Today? I don't think so. It was boiling hot all day, just like it was yesterday...yesterday! I remember now. It was cool in the morning, but by lunch it had heated up. I walked my bike over with Yanic and Melissa to the stage where they were serving our farewell lunch, then left the bike outside the stage, with both the green leather jacket I'd been wearing in the scene and my blue puffy coat draped over the handlebars. I wore the green leather jacket in a scene again today, so wardrobe must have picked up the blue coat too. Phew. They're still here packing up—Brittany probably sent it to the cleaners for me. But, in the wardrobe trailer, she tells me that when she grabbed the green wardrobe jacket from my bike yesterday, the blue coat wasn't there.

In all the years I worked there, I thought of the back lot as a sort of extension of my house. Since I often spent more time there than at my actual house, it made sense. But it's different on the lot now. Warner Brothers gives tours there now, which means it's much more crowded than it used to be, and there are a lot more people passing through. But still, throughout this whole shoot, I've left things all over the place and they've always come back to me. So I don't want to think the worst, but maybe tweeting that picture when the show was announced made it a desirable or fun collector's item for someone who was passing by? (By the way, if that someone is you, no hard feelings, but can you mail it back to my manager in Los Angeles, John Carrabino, no questions asked?) And for you at Scotland Yard, here's the last documented sighting of my blue coat:

It's just a coat, I know, but I held on to it for so long. I never wore it once after work ended on the original series, because how obnoxious would it be if you saw me wearing it in the grocery store, like, oh, oh, look at me! I wear a big puffy blue coat that says *Gilmore Girls*! I'm not even sure why I kept it. When I put it back on for the first time, there was a dried-out sugar packet in the pocket from 2008—I hadn't touched it since then. We once had a terrible winter of moths eating all our sweaters, but somehow they spared this coat— even they must have known I was going to need it again. For

Gilmore Girls: A Year in the Life, it was with me every day. It kept me warm and dry, and billowed out behind me as I rode my bike across the lot in the wee hours of night. So I can't help feeling a little sad it's gone.

But it's our last day, and the coat has served its purpose. Our work is over, and it's May in Los Angeles. The sun is blazing, and I don't need it to keep me warm anymore. Of course, for sentimental reasons I'd prefer to have it. But I think of the seventy incredible days of this shoot, all the people I'm so thankful for, all the love that went into making this show. I think of Emily in her Marie Kondo scenes, giving things away because she's learning a new way of being thankful for the past, realizing it's just as important to welcome and embrace the future. And while her scene is about *choosing* to give things away, rather than losing them or having them taken, in the spirit of what the book suggests I decide that, rather than mourn the loss of my jacket, I will be thankful for the time we had together. I thank it for hiding itself in the back of my closet with only a dried-up sugar packet to keep it company all those years. I thank it for standing by, for somehow letting me know I was going to need it again. I thank it for getting me through all seventy days of "Winter," "Spring," "Summer," and "Fall."

I thank it for all it did for me, and then I let it go.

After all, we waited a long time to get the chance to finish this show, and now, finally, *Gilmore Girls* is really and truly over.

I mean, it *is* over, right?

Yes. It is. It's over.

But seriously, didn't you sort of think that ending was really more of a cliffhanger?

Hmmmm ...

Acknowledgments

· ·

My literary agent, Esther Newberg, was one of the first to take a chance on me as a writer. I'm so thankful to her for her encouragement and for navigating me skillfully away from anything resembling *Monkey Doodles*.

I'm honored to have been able to work with the team at Penguin Random House once again. Thank you for your support: Gina Centrello, Kara Welsh, Jennifer Hershey, Kim Hovey, Cindy Murray, Susan Corcoran, Kristin Fassler, Shona McCarthy, and Paolo Pepe. I was thrilled to get to work with Sara Weiss for the first time. A special thanks to early readers Elana Seplow-Jolley, Anne Speyer, and Julia Maguire. Your input was invaluable and came at a time when I needed a boost the most.

Amy Sherman-Palladino gave me the role of a lifetime. I'll keep thanking her for that until the end of my days. I'm also thankful to the accidental writing school I got to attend thanks to years spent speaking her words, and those of Dan Palladino. I'm thankful to *all* the talented writers I've been lucky enough to work for as an actor in television and film, especially Jason Katims and the *Gilmore Girls* and *Parenthood* writing staffs.

Thanks to Helen Pai for going above and beyond.

Thanks to Elise LaPlante for her assistance during long days of filming, and for knowing how to set up the Friday night margarita bar.

I'm always grateful to my stellar team: Eddy Yablans, John Carrabino, Adam Kaller, and Cheryl Maisel.

Some friends whose early feedback always make it better: thank you, Kathy Ebel, Allison Castillo, Ellie Hannibal, and Mae Whitman.

My editor, Jennifer E. Smith, deserves all the thanks and praise I can possibly bestow. Our first book together was on a "rush" schedule, and this one was on something called a "crash" schedule. Not sure what's left, unless there's a "*San Andreas* starring The Rock" schedule. Through it all, she is generous with her intelligence, enthusiasm, and good taste, and I couldn't be more grateful. I am only saddened to have to inform her that, as a result of her excellence, she will never get rid of me.

Last but first is family. Especially in this process, I rely on my sister Shade Grant as a mentor, friend, and fashion advisor in equal parts (though the jumpsuits are not her fault). Thanks to the Grahams and Grants and Krauses and McHales and Morelands, especially the one who isn't here yet but whom I plan to soon spoil rotten. Thanks to Peter for taking such good care of me when writing moves in and eats up our regular lives.

Thanks to my mom and dad, where all the stories began.

ABOUT THE AUTHOR

Lauren Graham is an actor, writer, and producer best known for her roles on the critically acclaimed series *Gilmore Girls* and *Parenthood*. She is also the *New York Times* bestselling author of *Someday, Someday, Maybe*. Graham has performed on Broadway and appeared in such films as *Bad Santa*, *Because I Said So*, and *Max*. She holds a BA in English from Barnard College and an MFA in acting from Southern Methodist University. She lives in New York and Los Angeles.

@thelaurengraham

ABOUT THE TYPE

This book was set in Bembo, a typeface based on an old-style Roman face that was used for Cardinal Pietro Bembo's tract *De Aetna* in 1495. Bembo was cut by Francesco Griffo (1450–1518) in the early sixteenth century for Italian Renaissance printer and publisher Aldus Manutius (1449–1515). The Lanston Monotype Company of Philadelphia brought the well-proportioned letterforms of Bembo to the United States in the 1930s.